Contents

PART III

THE THEOPHANY: 38:1–42:6
THE SECOND POLE OF THE PROVERB:
HOW GOD SEES HIMSELF

Preface

To read any piece of serious literature one needs a coherent approach, an interpretative key. One does not read poetry as if it were prose. The *Book of Job* is widely recognized as a classic of world literature, not simply biblical literature. And it is timeless. Every generation has seen in it a work of unusual quality, of ever contemporary relevance. For it deals with the problem of the meaning of human existence in an often inhuman world. But it is immensely difficult, raising problems of style, structure, scope and authenticity. Perhaps part of its perennial fascination is due to its very difficulty of access, for it presents a challenge to the reader who looks to it for an answer to the problems of human life and intolerable suffering, injustice and alienation. Every reader sees in it a mirror of his own condition, and interprets it as such.

But what is the scope of the book? How does one read and understand it, given the complexity of its form, with its many possible additions made at various times by many different editors? Perhaps the best way of approaching the book is to see it as a whole, a literary artefact put together by an author-editor with a reader in mind. Thus a valid line of interpretation is to use literary categories rather than purely theological. There is a real dramatic quality to the work, and though certainly not "tragedy" or "drama" in any classical sense it has a perceptible quality of "the dramatic", and principles of tragedy can be applied. Its structure allows for this. A prose narrative sets the scene for a reader, presenting the human tragedy of an innocent and pious man struck down by suffering and loss. Two poetic sections follow. In the first, the victim reacts, evolving a personal argument in counterpoint with three minor

9

characters; and in the second, God responds in a theophany. So there is, visible to a reader, a skeleton structure that determines the way it is to be read: an opening scene, followed by an internal development of perception and thought communicated by means of a progressive dialogue between two major "characters", man and God, each presenting a point of view on the human situation. For this reason it may be useful to see it in terms of a Hebrew *mashal* or proverb with two poles that constitute a thesis and antithesis. The reader, knowing the situation of human alienation, follows two arguments as they unfold, one set over against the other, and comes to a personal conclusion regarding innocent suffering and the God who allows it. The best possible interpreter of the *Book of Job* is thus the individual reader.

Chapter 1

Purpose and structure of the Book of Job

Suffering is not the problem; God is. Without a belief in a personal God human suffering is simply a part of life, concomitant to the human condition. As such, it may be interrogated in the quiet way of academic speculation. An existential datum, it may serve the human mind as a sounding-board for more than one personal philosophy, and as such, of course, it is a universal symbol, a paradigm of man's fragility and his unending contest with his environment. At this level it may either be rejected or accepted with dumb resignation, as it has been in literary tradition from ancient Mesopotamia to the present day.[1] But taken in this spirit *it will not be felt*, it will not involve a reader. It will simply furnish a speculative touchstone for the interrogation of existence and a starting point for personal speculation. But for the believer it poses a major problem and sparks an intellectual crisis of faith. For if suffering is such a constant of human experience how can one continue to believe in a just God who is seen to visit suffering upon the innocent for no perceptible reason? From the opening chapters of the *Book of Job* it is evident that this is the critical question: *what kind of God* is it that allows the innocent to suffer, and indeed seems to cause that suffering?

The *Book of Job* is immensely difficult of access, and is commonly recognized as such by scholars of both secular and biblical literature. In the first place there is no simple "structure" as such, but there are many "internal structures" to be found: a structure of debate; one of "motifs", in which ideas such as "wish", "petition", "praise" occur; one of "repetition and variation".[2] Above all there is a dramatic structure of conflict and of progress towards an end.[3] In the second place two relatively unusual devices are used: two long units of reflective poetry are embedded in a prose narrative frame, and the poetry consists of extended dialogue, rather uncommon in the Old Testament, though frequently found in secular literature. Even within that dialogue the author makes use of a number of different literary genera, such as lament, monologue, disputation speech and lawsuit.[4] The hermeneutical problem caused by this complexity of style may in fact be what keeps this book within the ranks of world classics.[5] "Finding the meaning" becomes a personal challenge for every reader, and that means first finding the dominant literary genus and the basic structure.

"Every man his own interpreter" is true of *Job* as it is of most of the so-called "wisdom literature", in which category the book is usually placed. But what is meant by that particular label? While it is applied to a number of biblical books, mostly from the postexilic period (from the sixth century on), these have relatively little in common, and even Murphy's magisterial work of classification[6] does not harmonize such diverse works as *Proberbs* and *Job*, *Sirach* and *Song of Songs*; all technically "wisdom" genre, but sharing little more than the label. In fact, they form part of a larger body of literature belonging to the written tradition of Judaism, and are certainly different in kind to the more classic legal and prophetic traditions, which *do* have a certain common identity and a manifest theological function. Unlike these, "wisdom" is predominantly secular in its outlook, and apart from the later editorial additions to *Proverbs*, the *Book of Wisdom* and part of *Sirach*, has little overt theological interest. For the most part these books represent the literary efforts of the laity, and might better be viewed under the rubric of "the New Writers" – literature written by very different kinds of people over a period of five hundred years. They were, of course, believers, but what they wrote was primarily literature. What theology they contain comes indirectly, from their artistic vision rather than from revelation.

It is remarkably independent and self-contained as literature, and holds itself aloof from the purely theological traditions of Israel. It is also rather élitist, in that for the most part it is written by middle to upper-class laity: landed gentry, minor nobility and "university type" people who enjoyed considerable leisure, a certain standard of wealth and security and a remarkable degree of culture.[7] Aristocrats on their country estates, retired civil servants and teachers with a love of letters – one is inevitably reminded of ancient Chinese and Persian poetry, written by the same class of people with similar cultural interests and artistic preferences.[8] Indeed, its highly secular world-view and its literary sophistication point to its origins. For this reason it is singularly belletristic, and so is clearly distinguishable from the earlier, more confessional, literature. It was interested, as was Montaigne (another of the type), in "all that pertains to man", his life, his values, his aspirations; and so "religion" is seen more in terms of "goodness of life" than according to theological categories. In a way, it is concerned with building a truly human environment and establishing human standards. It projects a world in which the individual could live a full life, a world that would be creative of values.

For this reason one of its main intellectual premises was the concept of cosmic order – a belief that they shared with contemporary writers of diverse traditions: Egyptian literature with its concept of *ma'at* – the divine order that even the gods were subordinate to; and Mesopotamian writings whose equivalent was called ME. The "New Writers" of postexilic Israel held that the divine creator had established an ordered cosmos and that the truly "wise" person could integrate himself harmoniously into his environment. For this reason, any perceived failure of, or contradiction in, this pattern – such as the existence of meaningless suffering or the experience of absurdity – became the catalyst for intellectual exploration that could lead to scepticism (*Qohelet* and the *Saying of Agur* in Prov. 30:1–4) or open contestation (*Job*), expressed, of course, in artistic, and purely intellectual, terms.

As with the anonymous *Dream of a Rood*, Dante's *Divina Commedia* or T.S. Eliot's *Murder in the Cathedral* one does not question their religious content, but one does approach them as literature, using literary categories of interpretation. Like all great writers, what the writers of early Judaism offer is an artistic vision of the world of human experience. Because of this fact, the *Book of Job* is best interpreted as literature, according to established literary categories, and this means first discovering what type of literature we are dealing with.

The Book of Job as bi-polar proverb

One way to understand the book as a whole – which is the way the contemporary reader finds it as it is now presented in final form – is to see it as a bi-polar *mashal*, or Hebrew proverb with two contrasting options placed before an alerted reader: man's point of view presented in the poetic Dialogue that forms the first part of the book, and God's point of view presented in the Theophany that forms the second part. Notwithstanding the wide disagreement among authors as to the authenticity of many passages, including the wisdom poem of chapter 28, the Elihu speeches of chapters 32–37 and even the poems on Behemot and Leviathan that make up most of chapters 40 and 41, the *Book of Job* that presents itself for critical appraisal is the book as it now stands. This is the *opus* that must be interrogated, for it communicates a coherent artistic vision.

Seeing it thus as a whole, the bare bones of a skeleton do stand out, because very carefully presented. A prologue of two chapters sets the scene by establishing the actuality

14

of innocent suffering; this leads to a debate on the human condition, which in turn provokes a divine reaction. Thus the central structure consists of a Prologue (chapters 1–2), a Dialogue (chapters 3–31) and a Theophany in which God speaks his part (chapters 38:1–42:6), and these three sections carry the drama to its close. Thus, while redactional problems remain, a very clear *dramatic* movement manifests itself, as a human tragedy is exposed and two "characters" respond to it. From the very beginning the literary and dramatic character of the work stands out, and the movement of the "plot" is evident:

PROLOGUE
(*mise-en-scène*)
↓
2:11–13
(enter the minor characters)
↓
DIALOGUE
(God as he is seen by man)
↓
29–31
(man's challenge to God)
↓
THEOPHANY
(God as he sees himself)

The Prologue, then, often seen as editorially secondary, would appear to be *dramatically* necessary at the primary level, and this makes literary sense. Status is essential to tragedy[9] – queens, kings or gods: Clytemnestra, Oedipus, Prometheus, these are the very stuff of tragedy, as Steiner observes. What is required is moral status, because once this is postulated it can be assumed that the issues at stake will be important. The prologue to the *Book of Job* serves this purpose, presenting the hero to the reader as a paragon among mortals: "a man who was blameless and upright, who feared God and avoided everything evil" (1:1). When such a one is punished by the gods it raises questions about the gods. And the Prologue raises the same questions about Yahweh: what kind of divinity is this who is so easily

15

enticed into unjust action against a loyal servant? What kind of deity was Zeus, to pinion Prometheus to a rock for a kind action? The arrival of the friends in 2:11–13 provokes the first of two answers to the question:

> Now when Job's three friends heard of all this evil that had come upon him, they came each from his own place, Elphaz the Temanite, Bildad the Shuhite, and Zophar the Naamathite. They made an appointment together to come to condole with him and comfort him. And when they saw him from afar, they did not recognize him; and they raised their voices and wept; and they rent their robes and sprinkled dust upon their heads toward heaven. And they sat with him on the ground seven days and seven nights, and no one spoke a word to him, for they saw that his suffering was very great.

The entry onto to the scene of these three minor characters sparks the dispute, for they provide the conventional foil for the argument in which the protagonist presents his own conclusions, his own assessment of the divinity in an increasingly bitter and uncompromising series of speeches that culminates in a solemn declaration of innocence that challenges God (29–31). Both formally and structurally this oath calls for a counter statement[10] that duly arrives in a Theophany, where Yahweh responds by presenting his own point of view on the matter.

The Epilogue (42:7–17) solves nothing and offers no answer of the author's. It thus still leaves the need for an independent judgement, and this can be given only by the reader, for both Job and God are in litigation as plaintiff and defendant and are therefore involved in the action. A final solution simply does not exist *within* the *Book of Job*. What the reader is left with is, in fact, an open case that has yet to find a judgement: an innocent man has been crushed and harrassed; he presents his case, demanding a hearing and his adversary-at-law presents his defence. An open-ended *mashal*, in effect, a proverb in which a reader knows the background, hears the argument on both sides, and is called on to decide: who is "in the right", Prometheus or Zeus?

NOTES

1. Among Egyptian texts one can number the *Dispute over Suicide* and the so-called *Eloquent Peasant* from the third and second millennium B.C.; Mesopotamian literature includes *The Individual and his God* and the more famous "Babilonian Job", *Ludlul bel nemeqi* ("I will praise the Lord of wisdom). See M.H. Pope, *Job* (AB), New York, 1965, L ff. Among modern writers who have been influenced by the book one can number Kierkegaard's *Diaries*, Kafka's *The Trial*, Jung's *Answer to Job*. The book has had a significant influence on the modern existentialists, as can be seen in Camus' *Myth of Sisyphus*, Adamov's *Notes et Contre-notes*, Beckett's *Waiting for Godot* and *Endgame*, and Bloch's *Atheismus im Christentum*. See especially M. Esslin, *The Theatre of the Absurd*, New York, 1961 and D. Anderson, *The Tragic Protest*, London, 1969.

2. With R.A.F. MacKenzie, "Job", in *JBC*, 515. I prefer to ignore the "structure of cycles" that is traditionally held, since it is difficult to sustain throughout and falls apart at the so-called "third cycle".

3. See a series of articles by J.W. Whedbee, D. Robertson, L. Alonso Schökel, J. Crenshaw, J. Miles, in *Semeia* 7 (1977).

4. See D. Cox, "The Book of Job as Bi-polar Masal", in *Ant* 62(1987), 12–25. Also R.E. Murphy, *The Forms of the Old Testament Literature. Wisdom Literature*, Grand Rapids, 1981, 13ff, and C. Westermann, *The Structure of the Book of Job*, Philadelphia, 1981, and N. Habel, *The Book of Job* (OTL), London, 1985, 49ff.

5. G. Steiner, *After Babel. Aspects of Language and Translation*, London, 1975, " . . . the generation of obstacles may be one of the elements which keep a 'classic' vital".

6. R.E. Murphy, "The Concept of Wisdom Literature", in *The Bible in Current Catholic Thought* (ed. J.L. McKenzie), New York, 1962, 46–54, and "A Consideration of the Classification 'Wisdom Psalms' ", in *VIS* 9(1963), 456–467.

7. For a background to the literature of the period see M. Smith, *Palestinian Parties and Politics that Shaped the Old Testament*, London, 1987, 113ff; J.L. Collins, "Proverbial Wisdom and the Yahwist Vision", in *Semeia* 17(1980), 1–17; W.D. Davies & L. Finkelstein (eds), *Cambridge History of Judaism*, vol. 1, Cambridge, 1984.

8. One thinks of the teacher-civil servant in retirement who figures largely in *Proverbs*, especially 22–24 which is on the Egyptian model of *Amen-em-ope*; the retired priest-headmaster of a school that is *Sirach*, cf. B.L. Mack, *Wisdom and the Hebrew Epic*, Chicago, 1985; and the lady of quality who possibly gave us *Song of Songs*.

9. G. Brereton, *Principles of Tragedy. A Rational Examination of the Tragic Concept in Life and Literature*, London, 1968, 17.

10. R.A.F. MacKenzie, "The Purpose of the Yahweh Speeches in the Book of Job", in *Bib* 40(1959), 437.

17

PART I

THE PROLOGUE: 1–2
SETTING THE SCENE:
INNOCENT SUFFERING AND
A GOD OF JUSTICE

Chapter 2

The problem of God's responsibility: Job 1–2

> Once upon a time in the land of Uz
> there lived a man whose name was Job.

Already in the opening half-verse of the Prologue the reader realizes that he is entering the world of fable. Both the language, which is similar to that of the early patriarchal legends, and the formulaic style of the subsequent verses with its alternating numerical clichés ("seven sons . . . three daughters, seven thousand sheep . . . three thousand camels") confirms this, and breathes the atmosphere of popular legend.[1] Job is a classic hero of myth, not a real person. Not even the "Land of Uz" can be found on any map, though much effort has gone into the quest and much ink has been spilt on it. One might just as well search for the Land of Oz. What is more, the protagonist so introduced to the reader is a paragon, as the second half-verse immediately shows:

> that man was blameless and upright, one who feared God and turned away from evil.

To the atmosphere of fable established by v.1a there is now added a theological category, introduced into the description of the hero by four terms that are rich in biblical significance.[2] "Blameless" suggests personal wholeness or integrity as a human being – an integrity that extends beyond the personal to the social level – he is "upright" as well. Moreover, he is a figure of classic piety and religion:

"fearing God and turning from evil" – a double formula frequently used to describe religious faith and practice. He is a friend of God, clinically just to the point of being a laboratory sample. If this were not enough, he is also prodigiously wealthy and a veritable model of wisdom:

> He had seven thousand sheep, three thousand camels, five hundred yoke of oxen, and five hundred she-asses, and very many servants; so that this man was the greatest of all the people of the east.[4] His sons used to go and hold a feast in the house of each on his day; and they would send and invite their three sisters to eat and drink with them. And when the days of the feast had run their course, Job would send and sanctify them, and he would rise early in the morning and offer burnt offerings according to the number of them all; for Job said, "It may be that my sons have sinned, and cursed God in their hearts." Thus Job did continually.
>
> (1:3–5)

He is a hero of legend, and this fact establishes the tragic portent of what is about to happen – when adversity strikes such a one as this it is no mere human mischance but the fall of a titan, and the reader enters into the world of high tragedy.

It is eminently clear from the opening five verses of the Prologue that Job is destined to be the "suffering hero" of folk-tale, and as such he exemplifies the dilemma that faces the thinker in every age – the all too obvious fact that the innocent, the pious and the prosperous are victims of fate, often struck down and betrayed for no perceptible reason, as was the Oedipus of the Sophoclean trilogy. Job has been cast in the role of "Everyman", victim of the human condition of innate fragility and insecurity. But the author of the *Job* drama is more than a thinker and writer, he represents religious man, and so must go further, adding theology to his philosophy of the human condition. It does not "just happen" that the innocent suffer; God exists, he is lord of creation and has control of things. The world he has created operates according to his own established rules of equity and justice, and with such an ordered cosmic vision the suffering of the guilty can readily be accepted.

But Job is not guilty, he is a paragon of innocence. There-fore God is responsible: *he* is the one who allows the right-eous to suffer, and indeed may very well be the *cause* of such suffering. And in fact the author of the book is not talking about "innocent suffering", he is talking about divine culpability.

The author's additions to the folk-tale

The structure of the Prologue makes this clear. It is a careful editorial merging of two distinct strands, an old popular narrative combined with two episodes of the author's own composition, two scenes in heaven that depict a wager between Yahweh and the Satan.[3] It is noticeable that in these two scenes (1:13ff and 2:1ff) the divine name "Yahweh" is used. We are dealing here with the recognizable theological construct that is the God of Israel's religious tradition; a God we believe is just. The tension between traditional belief and experience is dra-matically presented: 1:1–5; 1:13–22 and 2:11–13 represent a familiar folk-tale in which a prominent and righteous person is inexplicably struck down by misfortune. He accepts this with patience, and his friends come to visit him with words of consolation and sympathy. But the author of the text that now constitutes chapters 1–2 has worked into this tradition two scenes that serve to point-up the real argument: in two successive meetings in the heavenly court the Satan tempts God into a foolish wager that results in the hero being struck, first by the loss of his family, then by personal sickness and pain.

1:1–5:	*Traditional.* A portrait of a legendary hero, pious and prosperous.
1:6–12:	*Author's addition.* A foolish wager in which Yahweh allows Satan have his way with Job.
1:13–22:	*Traditional.* Job is struck by a series of calamities that wipe out his family and property.
2:1–10:	*Author's addition.* A second encounter

> between Yahweh and Satan that
> reinforces the first and results in personal
> sickness.

The implications are clear. The *Book of Job* is not concerned with human suffering, but with Yahweh's responsibility for that suffering – for God knows quite well what he is doing. In 1:7–8 he recognizes Job's righteousness, using the same classic language of piety that is found in 1:1:

> Now there was a day when the sons of God came to present themselves before the LORD, and Satan also came among them. The LORD said to Satan, "Whence have you come?" Satan answered the LORD, "From going to and fro on the earth, and from walking up and down on it." And the LORD said to Satan, "Have you considered my servant Job, that there is none like him on earth, a blameless and upright man, who fears God and turns away from evil?" Then Satan answered the LORD, "Does Job fear God for naught? Hast thou not put a hedge about him and his house and all that he has, on every side? Thou hast blessed the work of his hands, and his possessions have increased in the land. But put forth thy hand now, and touch all that he has, and he will curse thee to thy face." And the LORD said to Satan, "Behold, all that he has is in your power; only upon himself do not put forth your hand." So Satan went forth from the presence of the LORD.
>
> (1:6–12)

It is Yahweh's assertion here that causes the trouble, and it is from this point that the movement develops.[4] The Satan's response purports to be an enquiry into the motive man has for his piety – self interest or disinterested love, which is it that keeps man faithful to God? While some authors hold that this is the purpose of the whole book, it seems unlikely in the face of the opening formula, which shows that it is precisely disinterested piety that marks the protagonist from the beginning.[5] This is substantiated by his own view of ethics in his final challenge in chapters 29–31. In fact, God himself confirms his first opinion of Job's fidelity in the second heavenly scene, 2:3:

And the LORD said to Satan, "Have you considered my servant Job, that there is none like him on the earth, a blameless and upright man, who fears God and turns away from evil? He still holds fast his integrity, although you moved me against him, to destroy him without cause."

Indeed, in this, his second boast in the Prologue, God appears to concede that to some extent he at least shares responsibility for what had happened "you provoked me to move against him",[6] he says rather defensively to the Satan, and indeed there seems to be something shame-faced about the divine admission, and this is coherent with the whole picture of Yahweh projected by the two additions to the folk-tale. Not only does he enter into a foolish and cruel wager with the Satan (1:12: "Very well, let us test a righteousness I am already sure of by inflicting psychological pain on an innocent man"), but the second time around he is duped by the Satan into going even further with the matter. Towards the end of the Prologue, as the friends come to console him, it is not Job and his suffering the reader wonders about, it is God; not the question of whether man's piety is disinterested or not, but the question of God himself. What kind of God is capable of allowing the innocent suffer for no valid reason? What kind of God is this Yahweh of Israel's experience? That the scope of the book is the elucidation of this theological problem and not the more philosophical one of the "why?" of suffering is confirmed by the use of the divine names. Only here in the Prologue is God called by his proper name, "Yahweh". Elsewhere in *Job* (apart from the Theophany where it reappears) one or other of the alternative names for the divinity are used: El, Eloah, Shaddai.

Belief in a divinity is one thing, and may be consonant with innocent suffering which can still be seen as a natural concomitant to the human condition. But a belief in Yahweh is a different matter, for with that one is in conflict with the whole theological tradition of a just God and a responsible, concerned creator. Thus the Prologue brings to the surface of the reader's perception the dangerous ambiguity in the traditional concept of Yahweh.[7] The fact is that the traditional theological categories have proved inadequate to cope with the "god" of human experience. Some innocent people suffer; that is the fact. And frequently the only one who can be seen to be responsible is God. The fact that the Prologue shows so clearly the degree of redactional work went into its composition is important. The poet of the final *Book of Job*[8] has reworked the old prose narrative of a just man struck by disaster to use it as a "setting the scene" for the rest of the book, and had it before him as he wrote, first the Dialogue, then the Yahweh Speeches. Being familiar with the folk-tale that was current in Near Eastern literature and known to his readers, he saw in it a point of departure for an existential theology, and inserted the "Satan episodes" of the wager with Yahweh as a dramatic device to sow in the minds of his readers the crucial question: "what kind of god is this one that so lightly allows an innocent friend suffer for no valid reason?", and more, "what kind of god could allow himself be tricked into making such a wager?" That this is the author's intention is clear from the juxtaposition of the "mythic hero" presented in the first verse and the formal repetition of Yahweh's acknowledgement of Job's integrity in the same classic formula. 1:8 and 2:3 put the opening formula of 1:1 in the mouth of God: "a blameless and upright man who fears God and turns from evil".

It is not the existence of suffering that is tragic, but the existence of a divinity responsible for this. By repeating the redactional formula of 1:6 ("One day the sons of God came to attend on Yahweh, and among them was Satan") in 2:1, thereby re-introducing the heavenly-wager scene, we are forced to look again at this scene.[9] And the addition of one word (Hebrew: *hinnam*, "for nothing") to the second question addressed by Yahweh to Satan shows where the author is leading the reader:

> The Lord said to Satan, "have you considered my servant Job, that there is none like him on the earth, a blameless and upright man, who fears God and turns away from evil? He still holds fast his integrity, although you moved me against him, to destroy him *for nothing*."

(2:3)

A rather feeble divine reproach, indeed, and already one begins to wonder about this divinity: indifferent? vacillating? unregarding of justice? one to whom loyalty means nothing? This rather sadistic experiment points to the fact that the author is about to embark on an enquiry into the sort of god capable of pushing a human being to breaking-point in a sort of macabre experiment. The strange character of Yahweh is what dominates the Prologue – God as he must appear to many people: uncaring, aloof, indulging in a private gamble with the well-being of his servant.

What kind of God is Yahweh?

The *Book of Job* is not about "justice" or about the suffering of the innocent: it is about God. It asks, "who is Yahweh?": the divinity as theological tradition depicts him – a "god" who is the mental construct of theologians? Or can one go further, can one really *know* the divinity in an existential sense – and if one did, what would one find? The Prologue thus puts a question-mark to Yahweh, the creator God of traditional theology whose personality fills the pages. He comes to the fore once again in a series of doxologies in the Dialogue (5:8f; 9:4f; 11:7f; 12:21f; 25–26) and he takes centre stage in the Theophany. But this creator-God, as the text-books portray him, is the god of cosmic order. He establishes the world and mankind in it; he orders and governs both according to his plan; he is *responsible* for it. Therefore the critical problem is his relationship with this world – and the question becomes larger: what kind of god could be responsible for the world *as we know it*? So the author's purpose in setting out the Dialogue and the Theophany that follow cannot simply be an exploration of suffering, of human piety, of justice or of faith. It cannot be the Satan's facile question: "is any man pious for nothing?" The problem is the personality of God *as he is experienced* – there appears to be something very wrong with *him*.

This question is coherent with the literary tradition of

the mythic hero: Oedipus dogged by a fate established by the heavens but unknown to him; Agammemnon forced by divine decree to commit a moral wrong (the sacrifice of Iphigenia, his daughter) for which he must inevitably be punished – by another divine decree; Job, a paragon of integrity allowed to suffer by a god who recognizes his integrity. The tragic element is present in all of these, and it underlines the fact that the real tyranny is not the injustice of man; it is the injustice of God, for this is a tyranny of the human mind.

If God is responsible, then one can understand why the *wicked* suffer. If man believes himself free of any divinity, then one can understand how *some* innocent suffer. But what explains the innocent who fall outside either category, and yet suffer? Does the created world answer to a law, or is it arbitrary? Again, the problem of the *created* world drives the thinker back to the source-problem: God; creator, ruler, judge – the traditional theological view of him. Or is there a different God, one who does not correspond to theological categories? As Paul Ricoeur observes,[10] suffering is a problem only when one believes in a god defined according to an ethical system of theology. The *Book of Job* recognizes this, for it lies within the tradition of Israel's ethical perception of God as responsible creator and legislator. But unlike much of that tradition it raises the problem that Yahweh, in his role of creator, is often incompatible with God the legislator. Man can see him in one or other of these roles, but it is difficult to see him as both at once – and the text-book theology of the schools failed to make this cohere in any adequate system. Given a world in which individual and social injustice exists; given the mystery of man's control of, and incapacity adequately to control, his own behavioural patterns; given also the enigma of man living in a world that, no matter how familiar, is ultimately alien – the real theological problem is the tension that lies between man and God as the tradition projects him.

In fact, many writers of the exilic and postexilic period, apart from Job, saw their own time as one marked by the failure of traditional modes of theology. The old, secure

28

belief in a divinely established world-order that could be perceived and co-ordinated in a theological system, and an equally secure belief that God was covenant God of Israel, was either rejected outright or seriously questioned. The "seminary text-books" were seen to be inadequate.[11] So Job, a layman educated in the secular mode, evolved a different theological method: a rational enquiry into God, based on experience illuminated by the intellect. There was nothing very unusual about this. The strength of Judaism, that which kept it flexible and capable of meeting new situations, was the tradition of lay study of theology.[12] Since the putative "theology of divine order" had failed to deliver, the individual was forced to go it alone and discover his own verities. To do this, the author of *Job* chose a literary form that was already familiar to the "wisdom" tradition – the Hebrew *mashal* or proverb. It is on this model that he structured his book.

The articulation of the Proverb of Job

If the whole of the *Book of Job* is a *mashal*, then it is necessary to understand its internal structure, the "How?" of its articulation as a book written for readers.[13] These know, as the three friends do not, that Job is a clinically just and innocent man. There can be no question in his case that suffering is the consequence of sin. Thus it is Yahweh who is on trial. The reader is waiting to see how the action of Yahweh in the Prologue can be justified. Job's dispute with the friends in the Dialogue (3–31) begins as a lament on the human condition, moves to an attack on the traditional theology of God and develops from there into an indictment of the divinity itself. From the beginning God is the defendant – or at least what is under attack is the theologians' view of him as creator, legislator and judge. Job is the plaintiff, arguing his case against the God of text-book theology – and his cause is that of Everyman. What the protagonist does is confront this "accepted truth" about the divinity with the "real" God of human experience: a cruel and deliberate destroyer of innocent human life; one who gratuitously oppresses his own creature and friend. Where does the defence rest? What is God's point of view? It is found in a rather ambiguous double speech in 38–41: a divine statement that in fact allows for as many interpretations as there are exegetes, for to a great extent Yahweh agrees with Job's basic assessment of the human condition as absurd, while on his part Job seems to accept the divine self-justification as valid: he "submits" (40:3–5 and 42:1–6) and in the Epilogue Yahweh publicly acknowledges that Job had after all "spoken of God what was right" (42:7), as against his own defence witnesses, Eliphaz, Bildad and Zophar, the textbook theologians.

The reader, who has been primed by his reading of the Prologue, is thus presented with a bi-polar *mashal* in which man's rational view of God is countered by God's view of himself.

DIALOGUE	YAHWEH SPEECHES
HOW MAN SEES GOD	HOW GOD SEES HIMSELF
an immoral manipulator who uses *force-majeure* to oppress his creature.	a transcendent creator whose operations are beyond man's comprehension.
To some extent God accepts this estimate:	To some extent Job accepts this estimate:
so Job's "rational theology" is vindicated.	so traditional theology is vindicated.

Faced with these two independent and parallel conclusions the reader is left to assess both arguments for himself and find his own response to the problem of "what kind of God?" posed by the Prologue.

This sort of "proposition" is familiar ground in biblical wisdom. The *mashal*, or proverb, is notoriously open-ended. It places before the hearer a thesis and an antithesis, two units parallel but different that build an inner tension of contrast, and leaves the conclusion to the personal judgement of the reader. That the *Book of Job* is *mashal* is confirmed by the ambiguity so frequently worked into the text by the author himself, and by the discrepancies deliberately written into it.[14] The Job of the Prologue is patient and submissive, while in the Dialogue he is a rebel; the friends of the Dialogue are loyal to the theological tradition, yet the God of the Epilogue repudiates them; the God of the Theophany challenges Job while the God of the Epilogue approves his stand. Even the Hebrew text frequently allows for contradictory interpretations. Then again, twice in the text the speeches of the protagonist are called *mashal* (27:1 and 29:1) and the Babilonian Talmud of later Judaism sees the Job-book as a *mashal*.[15] For the *Book of Job* the *mashal* form serves as a vehicle for involving the reader in the affair while at the same time making it clear that the decision must be made by a reader between the two theologies of God – that presented by the divinity and that of human reason based on experience.

The author does not supply answers – not necessarily because he could not but because his purpose in writing was to force the reader to think for himself in the light of his own experience. It is a poetic statement, and no systematic theology can be derived from such since reading poetry is, after all, an aesthetic experience, and so each reader is individually involved in an experience of human alienation and divine remoteness, and draws his own conclusions.

NOTES

1. The reader is immediately struck by the fact that the opening formula in Hebrew is not the usual one for historical narrative, as M.H. Pope observes: *Job. Introduction, translation and notes* (AB), New York, 1965, 3. I use this fact as justification for my translation. See also N.M. Sarna, "Epic Substratum in the Prose of Job", in *JBL* 76(1957), 13–25; S. Terrien, *Job* (CAT), Neuchatel, 1963, 51; N.C. Habel, *The Book of Job* (OTL), London, 1985, 34, and others.
2. J.L. Crenshaw, *A Whirlpool of Torment. Israelite Traditions of God as an Oppressive Presence*, Philadelphia, 1984, 58f.
3. See Pope's remark, *op. cit.*, LXIX: "The question naturally arises, why the devilish sadistic experiment to see if he had a breaking point?"
4. See Habel, *op. cit.*, 27.

5. R.E. Murphy, *The Forms of the Old Testament Literature. Wisdom Literature*, 20.
6. Pope, *op. cit.*, 20, and Crenshaw, *op cit.*, 60.
7. See W. Whedbee, "The Comedy of Job", in *Semeia* 7 (1977),7.
8. R.A.F. MacKenzie, "The Transformation of Job", in *BTB* 9(1979), 51.
9. Habel, *op cit.*, 28. Also H.H. Rowley, *Job* (New Century Bible), London, 1976, 34, and Pope, *op cit.*, LXIX.
10. P. Ricoeur, *The Symbolism of Evil*, Boston, 1967.
11. Biblical texts from this tradition include Prov.30,1–4; Ps.73; *Qohelet, Jonah* (see a study by B. Vawter, *Job and Jonah*, New York, 1983). For the dating of *Job* see L. Alonso Schökel, *Job. Comentario Teologico y Literario*, Madrid, 1983, 68f, and R.A.F. MacKenzie's argument, "The Cultural and Religious Background of the Book of Job", in *Concilium*, 1983, 3f. Also M. Smith, *Palestinian Parties and Politics*, 113.
12. *Op. cit.*, 112. See also H. Gese, "Wisdom Literature in the Persian Period", and M. Smith, "Jewish Religious Life in the Persian Period", both in *Cambridge History of Judaism* (ed. Davies & Finkelstein), 189–278. M.E. Stone (ed.), *Jewish Writings of the Second Temple Period* (CRINT), Philadelphia, 1984, 22f.
13. R.A.F. MacKenzie, "The Purpose of the Yahweh Speeches in the Book of Job", in *Bib* 40(1959), 437. Alonso Schökel, *op. cit.*, also speaks of the orientation of the whole book to a reader.
14. Y. Hoffman, "The Use of Equivocal Words in the First Speech of Eliphaz (Job IV–V)", in *VT* 30(1980), 114–119; W. Morrow, "Consolation, Rejection, and Repentance in Job 42,6", in *JBL* 105(1986), 211–225; and R.M. Polzin, *Biblical Structuralism. Method and Subjectivity in the Study of Ancient Texts*, Philadelphia, 1977.
15. See Pope, *op. cit.*, XXIX. The Targum–*Baba Bathra* 15a. See also Habel, *op. cit.*, 30, who however holds that the *mashal* in Job is not a traditional proverb as much as a formal pronouncement.

PART II

THE DIALOGUE: 3–31
THE FIRST POLE OF THE PROVERB:
HOW MAN SEES GOD

Chapter 3

The seeds of revolt

The God of the Prologue is a catalyst, only man's experience is real. Thus the starting point of an enquiry into the nature of God is the individual's assessment of the human condition as it has been experienced. This is the function of chapter 3, opening chapter of the Dialogue that forms the first pole of the proverb of *Job*. It is to this statement that the friends will respond, just as this is Job's first response to the experience of the Prologue. That for its part had proposed a working hypothesis, chapter 3 presents a man. If the "real" God is as he has shown himself in the first two chapters, then how can one respond to life as it is inevitably perceived: a prison of alienation created by the divinity? If things are as reason perceives them, then there is something very wrong with God.

The opening chapter of the first major section of the book introduces the real protagonist, and does so with dramatic force:

> After this Job opened his mouth and cursed the day he was born.
>
> (3:1)

The first, most spontaneous reaction to the experience of suffering and a God responsible for it is revolt. Not a disembodied revolt against circumstances, against an abstraction called "suffering", but a full-blooded revolt against the one responsible.

If the first verses of the Prologue presented the stereotype of the hero of myth, the opening verses of the Dia-

35

logue present a totally different picture – the reality of human suffering as it touches the individual; and the almost inevitable consequence – a sense of betrayal that grows into accusation and anger. Chapter 3 effectively presents a psychological portrait of the victim of disaster, carefully articulated in three steps: spontaneous lament, recrimination (the familiar sense of "why me?"), and anger – an anger that becomes clearly focused on the God who is responsible (v. 23).

The first part of the bi-polar *mashal* has begun, as is clear from the stylistic change of tempo – from prose to poetry, from folk-tale to curse and lament.[1] The patient Job has given way to the rebel, a more modern sort of folk-hero now replaces the traditional one. The story-line is broken, as Habel observes, but in one aspect of it the continuity is preserved: Job is still innocent, and God is still responsible for what has happened. The first thing one notes in this opening chapter of the debate is the fact that it is not really debate as such but a soliloquy on Job's part. He puts *to the reader*, rather than to the friends, the personal implications of his tragedy, and then universalizes them, going beyond personal experience to the perception that this is the lot of *all* mankind, born to fragility and absurdity. The theme of the Dialogues is thus established.

The structure of the soliloquy

The way this chapter is set out is interesting, for it foreshadows the way the argument of the whole of the Dialogue will move – from human experience to God, and this in turn will foreshadow the way the Yahweh Speeches will move – from God to human experience.

vv. 1–2:	An introduction that, by its verbal intensity, sets the tone for the whole chapter: "Then Job opened his mouth and cursed the day he was born".
vv. 3–10:	Articulates the curse, moving from a *personal* desire for oblivion to a more *universal* desire for cosmic oblivion.

vv. 11–19: A lament on the absurdity of Job's own existence, echoing and expanding the *personal* curse of the previous section.

vv. 20–26: A Lament on the absurdity of *human* existence in general, culminating in pointed accusation of the one perceived as responsible – God himself.

The first part of the soliloquy, the curse, opens with a tragic cry:

> Let the day perish wherein I was born, and the night which said, "a man-child is conceived."
>
> (3:3)

Not suffering, but life itself, is the problem: the unbearable obligation to go on living, to "carry on" with an existence that makes no sense and allows no reprieve of pain. The personification and doubling of the curse – day *and* night – establishes the immediacy and the personal nature of the tragedy. So great is his sense of loss and alienation that the day of his birth is seen as a personal enemy.[2]

But there is more here than simply a desire for death. Verse 4 expresses the wish that the day of his conception be consigned to darkness, "to the primordial condition of the world before creation", as Gordis[3] observes, and this reversal of creation and return to chaos is carried on into the next verses:

> Let that day be darkness!
>   May God above not seek it,
>   nor light shine upon it.
> Let gloom and deep darkness claim it.
>   Let clouds dwell upon it;
>   let the blackness of the day terrify it.
>
> (3:4–5)

The quality of myth that pervades these opening verses is obvious. Many authors have noted the similarity between this pericope and Jer 20:14–18, but Weiser notes that the power of this curse goes beyond the prophetic complain and approaches the domain of mythology. Even the language supplies an indicator. The prophetic curse uses the more usual word for imprecation, in Hebrew *'arûr*; Job uses the rather unusual verb *qalal*, which is typically directed against divinely ordained authority.[4] Already we have a dramatic foreshadowing of what is to follow: the Job of the Dialogue already appears as a man who is not going to be satisfied with half measures: Prometheus appears for the first time, and the scene is set for confrontation.

In v. 5 another interesting verbal form is used that reveals the almost schizoid attitude of the protagonist to the God he holds responsible: "May darkness and deep shadow *claim* that day". Here the verb translated "claim" (Hebrew *g'l*) is one that normally represents the *positive* action of God, but in this verse it is used negatively. This usage certainly intensifies the emotional nature of the curse, making it almost a non-rational, disorientated cry. But it also tells the reader how Job at this point views God. Also, in the parallel formed by v. 4 and v. 5 "darkness" (anti-creation) replaces God (creation) and is seen to be preferable to God – or at least to this "god" of meaningless suffering. With the use of such primordial imagery in the first verses it is clear that what follows in the rest of this curse (vv. 6–10) is more than poetic imagery.

> That night – let thick darkness seize it!
>   let it not rejoice among the days of the year,
>   let it not come into the number of the months.
> Yea, let that night be barren;
>   let no joyful cry be heard in it.
> Let those curse it who curse the day,
>   who are skilled to rouse up Levi'athan.
> Let the stars of its dawn be dark;
>   let it hope for light, but have none,
>   nor see the eyelids of the morning;
> because it did not shut the doors of my mother's womb,
>   nor hide trouble from my eyes.
>
> (3:6–10)

Weiser points out[5] that since the mythic language of Chaos is used, it appears that Job is treating, not simply of his personal alienation, but of the ultimate problems of human life in general, and is trying to respond to them in the language of myth. The curse is poetically addressed to the day (of birth) and the night (of conception) in such terms as to suggest that it is not simply his *own* birthday that preoccupies him, but the whole of a human life that is so miserable it had better never to have begun.[5]

In a leap of creative imagination the protagonist has passed from a perception of his own misery to a realization that this is in fact the essence of the human condition. Man has been arbitrarily cast into life by a God who equally arbitrarily causes suffering from which there is no escape. The cosmic nature of the curse in vv. 3–10 makes it clear that the human condition is what is in question. The prose introduction of vv. 1–2 had sounded a warning of what would happen in the three short poems that follow. They constitute a curse that moves from the personal to the universal, from empiric existence to existential *angst*. The "day of his birth" in v. 1 reappears in the opening verse of the first poem, v. 3, but then *immediately* follows a curse on *all* human existence (4–9). The "personal" appears again in v. 10, introducing a familiar existential image of "return to the womb",[6] and this dominates both the second poem (11–19) which also begins with the personal and moves to the universal, and the third poem which begins with the universal human condition (20–23), before coming full circle, back once more to the individual (24–26). Thus it would appear that this soliloquy, and the Dialogue for which it serves as a launching-pad, takes its meaning from the universal, and not from the particular. It is not simply Job that God has made a prisoner of existence, it is humankind: "Why make this gift of light to a man who does not see his way, *whom God hedges in on every side*?" (3:23).

Both the second and the third poem are introduced by the key word "why?" (in Hebrew *lammâ*), which serves to unite the two aspects of human misery under the one stylistic device of interrogative complaint.[7]

> Why did I not die at birth,
>> come forth from the womb and expire?
> Why did the knees receive me?

Or why the breasts, that I should suck?
For then I should have lain down and been quiet;
  I should have slept; then I should have been at rest,
with kings and counsellors of the earth
  who rebuilt ruins for themselves,
or with princes who had gold,
  who filled their houses with silver.
Or why was I not as a hidden untimely birth,
  as infants that never see the light?
There the wicked cease from troubling,
  and there the weary are at rest.
There the prisoners are at ease together;
  they hear not the voice of the taskmaster.
The small and the great are there,
  and the slave is free from his master.

                                   (3:11–19)

Job begins with what can be known – man's actual situation. He goes on from there to interrogate that which men call "God". Already he has taken up the classic existential position, for man is the only one who asks the question of the meaning of his existence, and therefore of his creator. That is his characteristic attribute as a human being: one who interrogates the concept "god". What began as an "explosion of a frustrated human being"[8] has become a philosophical enquiry into being itself and into the divinity. If conception and birth are a disaster, life is devoid of meaning, *and it is God who has so disposed it*. The use of the formal interrogative in v. 11, and its repeated use in the following verses, clearly marks a turning point in the soliloquy and in the attitude of the hero.[9] In particular the double "why?" that stylistically dominates the laments of 11–19 and 20–26, and thus also the curse of birth and human existence, is the leitmotif of man's philosophy of existence, and it ends with "why . . . God?", addressed to the origin of human alienation. For God has given life, unasked; he is the author of the absurd: "why make this gift of light to a man who does not see his way, whom God hedges in on every side?" (v. 23). He is thus the enemy of man (a theme Job will take up later in his debate with the friends), for he gives man life without a choice, a prison without an escape route. What is interesting is the way the second minor poem of vv. 11–19 shows how the hostility and the rage of vv. 3–10 have given way to what one might almost call a spirit of onthological curiosity.[10] Human life on earth is such a cruel and meaningless reality that the prospect of death becomes, at least momentarily, attractive. Verses 11–19 constitute an enquiry into the "peace of the dead", the state of non-being, which is seen as the only possible mode of release from the bitterness of forced labour. Indeed, the bitter servitude envisaged by these verses might very well make sense since there is some rationality to it, but the slavery of vv. 20–23 is beyond reason – for God is the taskmaster: he gave life (11–12), but made it harsh and sterile (20–23). The human creature is a prisoner of existence, an existence he himself did not choose. The author is deliberately playing off two ideas against each other: the state of non-being, first personal, then general (11–19), and the state of being, first general, then personal (20–26). But the whole is marked by a cruel crescendo of mental desolation, since the idea of death is all that Job can fix his mind on. He sees death as the negation, first of personal existence, then, as the concept expands, of human existence in general. Extinction is the only cure he knows for physical and psychological alienation.

A close reading of the final minor poem in this chapter reveals an interesting stylistic usage on the part of the author:

> Why is light given to those who grieve,
>> and life to those bitter of heart,
> Who long for a death that never comes,
>> and search for it more than men search for hidden treasure?
>> They would be glad to reach the grave,
>> and rejoice if they reached the tomb.
> Why is light given to one whose way is hidden,
>> one who has been hedged in by God.
> In place of bread I have only sighs,
>> and poured out like water is my groaning.
> That which I fear comes upon me,
>> and that which I dread befalls me.

No calm, no peace remains to me,
no rest have I but torment.

(3:20–26)

Verse 20 and v. 23 form an inclusion, "he who grieves" thus becoming parallel to "the one whose way is hidden [by God]". This is the key to the soliloquy, and it establishes the philosophico-theological viewpoint that is the subject matter of the Dialogue that follows. It categorizes God as the deliberate destroyer of meaning in life. The problem of human existence leads inevitably to the problem of God, at least for the believer. Also, the reader is impressed by the way the author leads up to his *coup-de-grace*: he begins rather indirectly with a simple "why?" (*lammâ* – v. 20), but this establishes continuity with the previous "why?" section (vv. 11–19), and God is not mentioned until v. 23. When he does finally introduce the divinity the author deliberately employs two words that reveal the way he is thinking: "one who has been hedged in by God". The verb sends the reader back to 1:10, where the Satan had claimed that God was protecting Job with a "hedge". Now Job uses the same image to accuse God of oppression. Habel, in a recent commentary,[11] sees this as dramatic irony, used to suggest two opposed conceptions of God – at once protector and oppressor. Also, the term used for "God" here is Eloah – not Yahweh, the specific name of Israel's theology. Eloah suggests rather the wider concept of "divinity", because the problem being addressed here is larger in its implications than Israel's faith. Here the real point of the *Book of Job* crops up again: why should God bother to give light (a synonym for life) to one whose way he hedges in, what kind of God would do that sort of thing? Job is obsessed by his inability to justify God's mode of action, an inability caused by his very justifiable doubts regarding God's "gift" of human existence.[12] It is this dilemma that provokes the Dialogue, true; but it is really the implication it holds that fuels the continuing debate for the "why?" of a God who acts in this way inevitably becomes the "What kind of God *could* act in this way?" This rational sequence is latent in the final

42

contrast between these verses (20–23) and the last pericope (24–26):

vv. 20–23: Life has no value for one "who is bitter of heart".

vv. 24–26: It is precisely this sort of life that God has given to me.

It is here, in the context of this fundamental question, that God is directly introduced.

Asking the "why?" of innocent suffering

In the Discussion that follows, the friends clearly see that Job is asking "the reason why", and they supply an answer: suffering is a consequence of sin. But this is a *religious* concept; it coheres with the text-books but not with life. It is due to a neat vision of the world, but Job does not share that vision any longer, and is forced to ask how the suffering of the innocent can be fitted into *any* rational vision of the world.[13] Once human existence is seen to be absurd, and its norms contingent, alienation becomes universal. The human condition does not fit into any reasonable scheme. It is thus that Job sees things, and he articulates his perception in this third chapter. It is a crucial statement and it sets the intellectual and psychological scene. The rest of the book flows from this, "It shows the inner realm in which it will unfold itself", as von Rad observes. The Dialogue, or at least Job's part in it, becomes an intellectual reaction to the situation as the protagonist sees it – the collapse of the rational grounds for "faith". For Job, as for Camus, "the stage-sets collapse", and the existential journey can begin.[14]

The author sets out with this clear idea, that there is no "divinely established" cosmic order that man can discover. Thus, finding himself in a meaningless universe, the best he can do is *create* for himself some corner of authenticity or rationality. The universe is always alien. Man, by making a moral choice humanizes it. Cleanth Brooks observes[15] that the Hemingway hero is doomed to defeat, but insists

43

on being defeated on his own terms. The Jobian author places his hero in the same position of awareness that the only "order" possible is one supplied by himself. In classic existential terms the choice is clear: suicide or revolt. Suicide is, of course one option for the existentialist, as Camus holds. But it is one Job had already repudiated when it was suggested by his wife (2:9: "Curse God and die"). More subtle, however, are the alternatives: intellectual or psychological suicide. The former means opting for a belief in a future life when all will be justified and made clear, but this choice is not possible within the author's Hebrew tradition that knows nothing of any life but this one. Psychological suicide involves a mute, animal acceptance of "the way things are". Both are latent in the lament of chapter 3, but they do not constitute the way Job goes. Instead, he chooses rebellion, another existential option and the matrix of literature. For Camus, the first ethical consequence of awareness of the absurd is an attitude of revolt, which is in fact a defiant rejection of all evasions and facile solutions which in the nature of things cannot satisfy the mind. Here man, faced with a cosmos he cannot rationally control, finds his true identity: in a consciousness of his capacity to rebel, what Camus calls a "metaphysical" rebellion, by which he means a revolt, not so much against the human condition as it is experienced as against the facile acceptance of text-book answers that do not fit the case but which nonetheless claim to determine the reality.[16] This is the artist's choice: creative anger. And it is Job's choice: not submission, not despair, but anger, and because of this the *Book of Job* deserves its classic status, for where there is anger there is humanity. W.B. Yeats insists[17] that violence is necessary for any activity that is to have meaning. Had Job not suffered unjustly would he ever have seen human existence in all its clarity? Had Grendel not existed, could *Beowulf* have been conceived? This is the genesis of epic – and one remembers that Milton saw *Job* as an epic. Job's anger comes from the betrayal of a clear, ethical vision: suffering makes sense if it responds to justice; if it does not fit into any pattern suffering is an

44

absurdity and God is more than incomprehensible – he is evil.

The reader, thus fortified in logic, now begins the theological discussion that is Job 4–14 with a *presumptio facti*: life is cruel and meaningless, therefore there is something wrong with God. The least one can say is that he is arbitrary – but what is the worst one can say? Verse 23 has set the tone; what follows comes naturally. As Job sees it, all of human life has been hedged in by God – he set its parameters and laid down its conditions. And this life is devoid of meaning, for no law of justice regulates it and the mind cannot encompass it. If the suffering he contemplates only made sense he could accept it as "simply the way things are" – but it is not amenable to reason. So the double question being asked in the chapters that follow (4–27) is: what sort of God is this one that does not correspond to the traditional concept, and how can the individual react to a meaningless life with integrity?

NOTES

1. N.C. Habel, *The Book of Job*, 102f, and R.E. Murphy, *Forms of the Old Testament Literature*, 22. For his part, Habel suggests that there is an element of poetry in the Prologue.
2. A. Weiser, *Das Buch Hiob. Ubersetzt and erklärt*, Gottingen, 1974, 39f.
3. R. Gordis, *The Book of Job: Commentary, New Translation and Special Studies*, New York, 1978, 32. See also Habel, *op. cit.*, 104f.
4. See A. Lefevre, "Malédiction et Bénédiction", in *DBS* V, 747. Also S.H. Blank, "The Curse, Blasphemy, the Spell and the Oath", in *HUCA* 23(1950–51), 73f and "Men Against God. The Promethean in Biblical Prayer", in *JBL* 72(1953), 1–13.
5. M.H. Pope, *Job*, 28. See also G. Ravasi, *Giobbe*, Rome, 1984, 328.
6. The concept of a return to the womb is common to most absurd writers. Being born into death is an image much used by the protagonist of Beckett's novel, *Malone Meurt*, Paris,1951. He was born into death and for him death at the end is some sort of womb: 114. The same image is used in the second act of his play *En attendant Godot*, Paris, 1952.
7. See C. Westermann, *The Structure of the Book of Job. A Form-Critical Analysis*, Philadelphia, 1981, 37f, and R.E. Murphy, *Forms*, 22.
8. N.C. Habel, *The Book of Job*, Cambridge, 1975, 20.
9. R.A.F. MacKenzie, "Job", in *Jerome Biblical Commentary* (ed.R.E. Brown et al.), London, 1968, 515.
10. S. Terrien notes how the author of *Job* goes further than the Hebrews in general in conceptual thinking, *Job, Neuchatel*, 1963, 65.

11. N.C. Habel, *op. cit.*, 52. See also G. Ravasi, *Giobbe*, 336.
12. See R.E. MacKenzie, *loc. cit.*
13. See P. Nemo, *Job et l'excès du mal*, Paris, 1981. Also F. Chirpaz, "Ernest Bloch and Job's Rebellion", in *Concilium* 1983, 23ff.
14. G. von Rad, *Old Testament Theology*, Edinburgh, 1968, I, 411. See also the work of A. Camus, especially *Le Mythe de Sisyphe*, Paris, 1942 and *La Peste*, Paris, 1947.
15. C. Brooks, *The Hidden God. Studies in Hemingway, Faulkner, Yeats, Eliot and Warren*, New Haven/London, 1963, 10f.
16. See A. Camus, *Mythe de Sisyphe*, 118. See also for a discussion of this existentialist perception in Camus, Kierkegaard and Prometheus D. Anderson, *The Tragic Protest. A Christian Study of Some Modern Literature*, London, 1969, 83 and J. Cruickshank, *Albert Camus and the Literature of Revolt*, Oxford, 1970, 70.
17. W.B. Yeats, *Under Ben Bulben*, 111. See also P. Ricoeur, *The Symbolism of Evil*, 290f.

Chapter 4

A rational enquiry into God

The absurdity of the human condition established by chapter 3 triggers the debate between Job and the friends, for it presents the cosmic contingency of man's situation in a world in which moral values no longer apply, since it is evident that a "just" God perverts justice and an "innocent" man is driven to pray for annihilation. It is to this position that Eliphaz immediately addresses himself in chapters 4–5, thus opening the discussion. There is no doubt that at the outset he means to be consoling – his argument is courteous and restrained. He recognizes the fact that Job is an exceptionally good man (4:3–4) and reassures him that his painful situation is not irremediable, for traditional theology has much to say that is positive on the matter of suffering. It knows that ultimately the righteous do not perish (vv. 7–11), and the theologian realizes that what is happening to Job could happen to anyone. So far, albeit unconsciously, he is in agreement with Job's statement in chapter 3, but his reasons are different: simply, no one is *so* righteous that he can expect his life to be totally free of suffering; since all are sinners suffering must be part of everyone's lot. Job is no exception. Once he accepts this fact he may be sure that God will restore him to accustomed well-being, after he has been "re-educated" *by a period of suffering commensurate to his sinfulness*. But it is precisely *this* argument that shows up the intellectual weakness of this first friend's position to the extent that, unperceived by himself, he is laying the groundwork for what will be the major rebuttal of the protagonist: *commensurate* suffering would be reasonable.

Opening the debate

The debate begins here with Eliphaz representing the traditional theology of a just God, and he makes the major point of his theology of God for the first time – a doctrine that will run through all his subsequent contributions to the debate and one that was familiar to thinkers even outside Israel.[1]

> Think now, who that was innocent ever perished?
> > Or where were the upright cut off?
> As I have seen, those who plough iniquity
> > and sow trouble reap the same.
> By the breath of God they perish,
> > and by the blast of his anger they are consumed.
> The roar of the lion, the voice of the fierce lion,
> > the teeth of the young lions, are broken.
> The strong lion perishes for lack of prey,
> > and the whelps of the lioness are scattered.
> Now a word was brought to me stealthily,
> > my ear received the whisper of it,
> Amid thoughts from visions of the night,
> > when deep sleep falls on men,
> dread came upon me, and trembling,
> > which made all my bones shake.
> A spirit glided past my face;
> > the hair of my flesh stood up.
> It stool still,
> > but I could not discern its appearance.
> A form was before my eyes;
> > there was silence, then I heard a voice:
> "Can mortal man be righteous before God?
> > Can a man be pure before his Maker?
> Even in his servants he puts no trust,
> > and his angels he charges with error."

(4:7–18)

Indeed, Job himself accepts this argument, but simply as a stalking-horse, for he answers it later on in 9:2f and

48

ultimately challenges its validity in 14:1f. For the simple fact is that the argument of "no one being righteous before God" unfortunately implies the matching doctrine of commensurate suffering, which is accepted dogma to Eliphaz,[2] but which for the protagonist and the reader founders on the reef of experience. Indeed, the reader should already have recognized the clues: he has already been told in the opening verse of the "black fable" that is the book that Job is the perfect religious person described in terms of classic piety: "blameless and upright, fearing God and shunning everything evil" (1:1). And even though Eliphaz puts it more elegantly, there is little to choose between his argument and that of the Satan in the Prologue: both propose a self-serving ethic of earning a reward by dint of piety. A reader taking careful note of the overall structure knows where he stands.

The argument cannot be valid, for Job is, by author's intention, a clinical test-case of righteousness from the first moment of the action. Even if this were not so, and 1:1 had not set the "laboratory" atmosphere, the logic would still falter, as Job sees for himself in the next speech, particularly in chapter 7: all men have indeed a "hard service here on earth" (v. 1), but why should God torture *him* beyond measure? (v. 19).

> Therefore I will not restrain my mouth;
>   I will speak in the anguish of my spirit;
>   I will complain in the bitterness of my soul.
> Am I the sea, or a sea monster,
>   that thou settest a guard over me?
> When I say, "My bed will comfort me,
>   my couch will ease my complaint,"
> then thou dost scare me with dreams
>   and terrify me with visions,
> so that I would choose strangling
>   and death rather than my bones.
> I loathe my life; I would not live for ever.
>   Let me alone, for my days are a breath.
> What is man, that thou dost make so much of him,
>   and that thou dost set thy mind upon him,
> dost visit him every morning,

and test him every moment?
How long wilt thou not look away from me,
   nor let me alone till I swallow my spittle?
If I sin, what do I do to thee, thou watcher of men?
   Why hast thou made me thy mark?
   Why have I become a burden to thee?
Why dost thou not pardon my transgression
   and take away my iniquity?
For now I shall lie in the earth;
   thou wilt seek me, but I shall not be.

                                 (7:11–21)

The author is taking up the flaw in Eliphaz's argument, for admittedly *no* one is righteous – but only *some* suffer! It is more than a question of all men being born to pain, as Eliphaz the theologian held (5:7); in Job's own case this is not simply the working out of a law of nature: the "retribution" he experiences is excessive. God is actively his oppressor, over-reacting to human weakness (7:20). Job is not simply answering his interlocutor, he is developing his own assessment of the situation, bringing together his own experience and Eliphaz' argument and drawing out the logical implications. The reader, knowing what others do not (the calibre of the protagonist) sees further than Job can as yet do. Job's answer to traditional theological categories has to do with the *excess of suffering*; human experience shows it is not condign, therefore it is (according to human reason) unjust, and (recalling 3:23) God is responsible for it. Knowing this, one is driven by logic to question just how strange God is – for he seems to be much more than arbitrary; he is a "watcher of men".

Chapter 8 sounds the first note of intolerance as Bildad, the second friend, opens up by ridiculing Job's argument. The formal style betrays the intention: technically a "disputation speech" it in fact goes beyond accepted norms, becoming litigation, pure and simple.[3] Bildad reiterates the tradition enunciated by Eliphaz – that misfortune is the result of moral iniquity (8:8), but the reader notices a subtle re-drawing of battle lines. The second friend raises a question that Job has not so far posed in explicit terms: the justice of God. It is perceptive of him, for that is simply one further step on Job's rational journey, already implicit in his argument of God's arbitrariness. God *is* just, Bildad asseverates, and tradition will amply bear this out:

> Then Bildad the Shuhite answered:
> "How long will you say these things,
> and the words of your mouth be a great wind?
> Does God pervert justice?
> Or does the Almighty pervert the right?
> If your children have sinned against him,
> he has delivered them into the power of their trans-
> gression.
> If you will seek God
> and make supplication to the Almighty,
> if you are pure and upright,
> surely then he will rouse himself for you
> and reward you with a rightful habitation.
> And though your beginning was small,
> your latter days will be very great.
> For inquire, I pray you, of bygone ages,
> and consider what the fathers have found;
> for we are but of yesterday, and know nothing,
> for our days on earth are a shadow.
> Will they not teach you, and tell you,
> and utter words out of their understanding?
> Can papyrus grow where there is no marsh?
> Can reeds flourish where there is no water?"
>
> (8:1–11)

The spark is in the stubble, for this is enough to set Job thinking independently, pushing his own reasoning one step further, well beyond anything the friends could have considered. If God *is* arbitrary, and if he is seen in fact to use *force majeure* against man, this in itself points to an "unreasonable" God, or at least an "un-human" one. But there is more, for increasingly he is seen as a divinity deliberately hostile to Job, and so to man – his own creature. This development places chapters 9–10 among the most critical in the book, as the protagonist sums up the argument from the beginning, and the accusation against God, first suggested in chapter 3, is intensified through the intervening chapters to reach its peak in 9–10.[4] Job repeats Eliphaz's thesis,[5] but he also dares to define the creator in

51

his own terms. If it is true that no mortal can be righteous before God (9:2) this simply underlines the disreputable side of God's character. In his actions he reveals himself as one who is willing to resort to crude bullying, hounding man and free to act as he wishes.

> Then Job answered:
>   "Truly I know that it is so:
>   But how can a man be just before God?
> If one wished to contend with him,
>   one could not answer him once in a thousand times.
> He is wise in heart, and mighty in strength
> – who has hardened himself against him, and succeeded? –
> he who removes mountains, and they know it not,
>   when he overturns them in his anger;
> who shakes the earth out of its place,
>   and its pillars tremble;
> who commands the sun, and it does not rise;
>   who seals up the stars;
> who alone stretched out the heavens,
>   and trampled the waves of the sea;
> who made the Bear and Orion,
>   the Pleiades and the chambers of the south;
> who does great things beyond understanding,
>   and marvellous things without number.
> Lo, he passes by me, and I see him not;
>   he moves on, but I do not perceive him.
> Behold, he snatches away; who can hinder him?
>   Who will say to him, 'What doest thou?'
> God will not turn back his anger; beneath him bowed the
>   helpers of Rahab."
>
> (9:1–13)

Job cannot see him as a God who listens or with whom one can argue; he is not answerable to reason. Rather is he cruel to just and unjust alike. What is strange is that while the protagonist already sees this point he keeps on trying to make God toe the line of logic. But the gap between God and man – and man's concept of him – remains:

> How then can I answer him,
>   choosing my words with him?

52

Though I am innocent, I cannot answer him;
  I must appeal for mercy to my accuser.
If I summoned him and he answered me,
  I would not believe that he was listening to my voice.
For he crushes me with a tempest,
  and multiplies my wounds without cause;
he will not let me get my breath,
  but fills me with bitterness.
If it is a contest of strength, behold him!
  If it is a matter of justice, who can summon him?
Though I am innocent, my own mouth would condemn me;
  though I am blameless, he would prove me perverse.
I am blameless; I regard not myself;
  I loathe my life.
It is all one; therefore I say,
  he destroys both the blameless and the wicked.
When disaster brings sudden death,
  he mocks at the calamity of the innocent.

(9:14–23)

So far God has appeared to human reason as arbitrary
and cruel. Now (in 9:32) comes a hint of his injustice. Job
takes up the question of "divine injustice" but treats it
more seriously than do the friends, for to him it seems
beyond all logic, all human thinking. God establishes his
own moral categories, based on whim – Caliban upon
Setebos. While this takes up Bildad's argument (from
chapter 8) it does so from a different point of view. It is
not so much that God *perverts* justice as that whatever he
does must be defined as "justice". And Job is learning
"fear", but a different kind to the "theological fear" he
began with (1:1). When he tries to approach *this* newly
perceived divinity he fails. Indeed, from here on Job tends
to underline the blatantly irrational aspect of God's
activity.[6] His interventions in human life are inexplicable.
In the rest of the Dialogue, perhaps, one may speak of
"characterization", as the theological development is
enhanced by psychological shading. Job has entered fully
into the persona of a character of the absurd, and shows
the characteristics of such: throughout the rest of the
debate tolls the constant bell of mortality
– "my days run hurrying by, seeing no happiness in their

flight, skimming along like a reed canoe . . ." (9:25f); "fear comes over me at the thought of all I suffer" (9:28); "Since I have lost all taste for life . . ." (10:1). The human condition, rather than the individual experience of alienation is the dominant factor, and it is this perception that pushes Job fully into a recognition of the fact that God is more than irresponsible. He is malicious. This is the only rational judgement one can make.

Do God and man have anything in common?

This new note appears in chapter 10 which is a cry for judgement – that is, for the restoration of rational principles in the God-man relationship. It embodies a powerful accusation against God: he created man, and seemingly not without effort! Yet he goes to equal trouble to make this creature suffer. More, one begins to suspect that during the very process of creation he harboured ill-intent:

> Thy hands fashioned and made me;
>   and now thou dost turn about and destroy me.
> Remember that thou hast made me of clay;
>   and wilt thou turn me to dust again?
> Didst thou not pour me out like milk
>   and curdle me like cheese?
> Thou didst clothe me with skin and flesh,
>   and knit me together with bones and sinews.
> Thou hast granted me life and steadfast love;
>   and thy care has preserved my spirit.
> Yet these things thou didst hide in thy heart;
>   I know that this was thy purpose.
> If I sin, thou dost mark me,
>   and dost not acquit me of my iniquity.
>
> (10:8–14)

The import of v. 13 is clear: "Yet, after all, you were dissembling, biding your time, I know". In the first step of the argument (6–9) Job was simply probing the traditional concepts of God and man and forcing the conclusion that God was arbitrary. But if the implications are drawn out the second step must be an awareness of malice, because as Camus observes, if God *is* God *he is responsible.*[7]

As a unit chapter 10 charts an interesting development in the thought of the book as the protagonist enters upon the second stage of his existential journey. Up to this there have been questions; now Job begins to realize *that there are no answers* and, slowly at first, he begins to slough the commonly held theological beliefs about God. "Does God see through human eyes? Does God share man's way of looking at things?"[8] is now the question (10:4). Are both God and man on the same, or even comparable, wave-lengths? By implication the question has become sharper: "can *man see God* through human eyes? If he looked at him that way *what would he see*?" God is the sort of divinity that punishes both wicked and good. He would punish Job no matter which he were: "If I am guilty, woe to me! Even if I am innocent . . . I am drowned in my affliction" (10:14–15). And if this is true of one person it is true of any person. Already the rational view of God is become more acute: if God would afflict anyone, irrespective of merit, and even project a long-term campaign of torment, he is a savage divinity. God's attitude is more than coincidence. He is constantly alert for some opportunity to hurt his creature. This idea is now expanded in vv. 18–22, a clear reprise of 3:20–23. God lacks any trace of human compassion: "let me alone, that I may find some brief comfort before death" is just one more in a series of hopeless prayers to this ruthless creator that is designed to quicken the pulse of human drama.

What is decidedly noticeable in chapter 10 is the hardening of the verbs, a stylistic adapted to showing a growing clarity of perception with regard to God.

> If I am wicked, woe to me!
> If I am righteous, I cannot lift up my head,
> for I am filled with disgrace
> and look upon my affliction.
> And if I lift myself up, thou dost hunt me like a lion,
> and again work wonders against me;
> Thou dost renew thy witnesses against me,
> and increase thy vexation toward me;
> thou dost bring fresh hosts against me.
>
> (10:15–17)

This is the high point of rational man's perception of deity. With it begins also the first hint, as yet lightly drawn, of the demand for a trial, "Job versus God", that later dominates the speeches of the protagonist. "I will say to God, 'do not condemn me, but tell me the reason for your assault' " in 10:2 is no more than a fleeting reference to a legal dispute (in Hebrew, *rîb*), but it prepares the way for the "lawsuit" theme that plays an increasing role in the Dialogue from now on.

In the first exchange with Eliphaz (chapters 4–7) Job's divergence from the tradition held by the friends had not been too radical. There was much they all agreed on: God's omnipotence, his omniscience, his transcendence. But by chapters 9–10 Job has broken radically with traditional theology and is poised for a free-flight of his own: God is all of the above, which is simply to say he is God: he has power and knowledge – but he grossly misuses both, and has always done so. The structure of this speech is fascinating. Job begins in 9:5–24 with a doxology on God's creative power and superiority over man, reaching its high point with the conclusion in vv. 22–24 that he is answerable to no moral law whatever. This is then developed in a reflective meditation on God and his relationship with man, 9:25–10:1a. He ends the speech with an accusation addressed *to* God, 10:1b–22. The whole represents a harsh transition from doubts *about* God's way of dealing with his creation to a direct accusation *against* him of the criminal misuse of power: "if I make a stand, like a lion you hunt me down, and work your fearful power against me again and again. You increase the number of witnesses against me; you grow in anger against me".

Thus in chapter 10 Job has done the unforgivable: he has speculated about God and drawn purely logical conclusions. Neither Eliphaz (4–5) nor Bildad (8) would have even considered it possible; Zophar, however, now recognizes where Job is headed and explicitly condemns the process:

Then Zophar the Naamathite answered:
"Should a multitude of words go unanswered,

and a man full of talk be vindicated?
Should your babble silence men,
    and when you mock, shall no one shame you?
For you say, 'My doctrine is pure,
    and I am clean in God's eyes.'
But oh, that God would speak,
    and open his lips to you,
and that he would tell you the secrets of wisdom!
    For he is manifold in understanding.
Know then that God exacts of you less than your guilt
    deserves.
Can you find out the deep things of God?
    Can you find out the limit of the Almighty?
It is higher than heaven – what can you do?
    Deeper than Sheol – what can you know?
Its measure is longer than the earth,
    and broader than the sea.
If he passes through, and imprisons,
    and calls to judgment, who can hinder him?
For he knows worthless men;
    when he sees iniquity, will he not consider it?
But a stupid man will get understanding,
    when a wild ass's colt is born a man."

(11:1–12)

Here the third friend is simply voicing the common doctrine that God is to be accepted – not subjected to rigorous logic! And Job is claiming that his *doctrine* is pure. The Hebrew text of v. 4 ("my way of life is flawless") in fact reads *zak liqhî*, "my beliefs, my teaching", so implicitly Zophar has recognized the fact that Job has developed a *formal teaching* – that he is now presenting a *doctrine*. His reaction is immediate – and predictable: God's nature is beyond human understanding; he could vindicate himself if he chose to do so (vv. 5–6) for he does deal righteously with both just and wicked. He is transcendent: a mystery to be acknowledged, not plumbed. This is the heart of Zophar's argument in vv. 7–12, but the remonstrance has come too late, for Job has gone beyond the question of God's equity and is concerned more with his malice and cruelty. For Zophar, man cannot know God and, by implication, should not speculate about him either

– in v. 10 the third friend introduces the "lawsuit" theme to show that God is above it all. But for Job himself thinking about God is the only sane response to absurdity. What is more, he has the firmest basis for the process: experience and reason. The friends have presented the theoretical "God" of theology; Job for his part insists on presenting the existential God of human experience. While holding to traditional categories – God as creator, lord of history and judge – he sees them simply as a tradition to be interrogated rather than accepted. It is precisely this "sapiential" argument that he now puts forward in chapters 12–14.

Questioning the concept "God"

The fourth Jobian speech is an answer to no one friend in particular. While it embraces all of them it really serves as a summary statement of where Job has arrived in his personal enquiry into God. They had all begun with the same tradition of an omnipotent creator (12:13–25), but in the face of common experience of life where does one go from there? Indeed, to the thinker there may even be something a little unsettling about his lordship[9]:

> Who among all these does not know
>   that the hand of the LORD has done this?
> In his hand is the life of every living thing
>   and the breath of all mankind.
> Does not the ear try words
>   as the palate tastes food?
> Wisdom is with the aged,
>   and understanding in length of days.
> With God are wisdom and might;
>   he has counsel and understanding.
> If he tears down, none can rebuild;
>   if he shuts a man in, none can open.
> If he withholds the waters, they dry up;
>   if he sends them out, they overwhelm the land.
> With him are strength and wisdom;
>   the deceived and the deceiver are his.

He leads counsellors away stripped,
  and judges he makes fools.
He looses the bonds of kings,
  and binds a waistcloth on their loins.
He leads priests away stripped,
  and overthrows the mighty.
He deprives of speech those who are trusted,
  and takes away the discernment of the elders.
He pours contempt on princes,
  and looses the belt of the strong.
He uncovers the deeps out of darkness,
  and brings deep darkness to light.
He makes nations great, and he destroys them:
  he enlarges nations, and leads them away.
He takes away understanding from the chiefs of the people
    of the earth,
  and makes them wander in a pathless waste.
They grope in the dark without light;
  and he makes them stagger like a drunken man.

(12:9–25)

The traditional truths are banalities, and if the friends really faced up to what they know about him they, in common with the whole of creation (vv. 7–9) would have to agree. Chapter 12 is more than a satire,[10] and more than simply a condemnation of the theology of the friends. It plays a much more crucial role in the drama. In chapters 12–13 Job presents an argument based on *personal* experience, as against the inherited wisdom of the friends. The argument is carefully layered:

12:2–6:	personal experience of God
12:13–25:	classical wisdom about God
13:1–5:	a new, "minor" speech that again proceeds from experience.

In all probability this last pericope is meant by the author to function as a transitional link, marking Job's movement away from debate with the friends to open confrontation with God.

Lo, my eye has seen all this,
  my ear has heard and understood it,
What you know, I also know;

> I am not inferior to you
> But I would speak to the Almighty,
>   and I desire to argue my case with God.
> As for you, you whitewash with lies;
>   worthless physicians are you all.
> Oh that you would keep silent,
>   and it would be your wisdom!

(13:1–5)

Certainly, the whole speech (12–14) is a clear attack on God as he presents himself to reason. He is not a God of justice, nor even an indifferent one; he is a purveyor of pain, an agent of cruelty. It is not simply, and universally, a case of cause-effect (as the friends hold); man's suffering does not just come about – *God does it*. Even if he were a "just" divinity in the way the friends see him, what an inhuman being he would be, for even a just human being is above measuring out one's meed (as Job shows is true of himself in 29–30).[11] In fact, the application of rational principles to the evidence of God's treatment of the world has nothing to say about man's ethical status – all it can tell one about is God and his non-human ways. He cannot be defended because he cannot be explained in human terms, and this is the mistake all three friends make. The question remaining is, "how are we to understand the God of human experience?" It is noticeable that the tradition in question is not as such traditional *theodicy* as it is the traditional concept of God. And since the friends are repelled by the idea of speculating about the divinity (though they share Job's own premises of experience and tradition, 13:1–20) he now tries out his thinking on God himself.

Complaint about God is now replaced by lawsuit[12]; God is called on to explain himself, to justify his way with creation. It is argued[13] that chapter 13–14 introduce an attitude of hope – Job expecting to heal the breach between himself and God by the intensity with which he appeals for "vindication" (13:14ff). But even the immediate context belies this. The confidence of this speech – if it is confidence – does not last. The further Job travels on from his first premise the weaker grows his "hope". He must eventually realize that the condition he lays down cannot be met:

"Only grant two things to me . . . withdraw your hand far from me, and let not dread of you terrify me" (13:20f). And in his heart he already knows this (vv. 24–27). As a result, chapter 14 presents itself to the reader as a reprise of chapter 3, with 14:5–6 taking up the theme of 3:16–19. But it carries the monologue of chapter 3 one step further: there is no cure for the present situation to be found in the future (14:7ff). *The present human condition is the permanent human condition.* What is often taken to be "hope" in these chapters is no more than the inarticulate cry of a trapped animal, as the development from vv. 13–17 to vv. 18–22 demonstrates.

> Oh that thou wouldest hide me in Sheol,
> > that thou wouldest conceal me until thy wrath be past,
> > that thou wouldest appoint me a set time, and remember me!
> If a man die, shall he live again?
> > All the days of my service I would wait,
> > till my release should come.
> Thou wouldest call, and I would answer thee;
> > thou wouldest long for the work of thy hands.
> For then thou wouldest number my steps,
> > thou wouldest not keep watch over my sin;
> my transgression would be sealed up in a bag,
> > and thou wouldest cover over my iniquity.
> But the mountain falls and crumbles away,
> > and the rock is removed from its place;
> the waters wear away the stones;
> > the torrents wash away the soil of the earth;
> > so thou destroyest the hope of man.
> Thou prevailest for ever against him, and he passes;
> > thou changest his countenance, and sendest him away.
> His sons come to honour, and he does not know it;
> > they are brought low, and he perceives it not.
> He feels only the pain of his own body,
> > and he mourns only for himself.

> (14:13–22)

The "but" of 14:18, in the original text, serves an adversative function. It reverses the thrust of the previous five verses. If indeed vv. 13–17 had expressed a hope it could have been no more than the mind's galvanic recoil from the pain of existence: "you destroy man's hope . . . he feels but the pain of his own body" (vv. 19 & 22a). There is no question of man deserving what he gets, he is weak by nature and simply cannot "be just before God" (vv. 1–3). But God for his part could afford a little compassion; this would be humanly comprehensible (v. 6) – "turn your eyes from him, leave him alone, like a hired drudge, to finish his day" – but there is neither further hope (vv. 7f) nor a present respite (vv. 20f): "you destroy him, and forever he is gone".

As a response to Eliphaz (which it is) it is late, but it serves here as a conversational full-stop: the traditional way of looking at God is inadequate, and Job must now go his own way to the end. He has asked God for justice, or at least for pity, but God turns an inhuman face to his need (13:24), not even granting a temporary release before death intervenes.[14] After that it will be too late, for death spells extinction. Job has been genuinely dedicated to God with a disinterested love. This was made clear to the reader, first in the Satan's intervention in the Prologue and then in the protagonist's own "oath of clearance" in 29–31. But now it is evident (to the reader) that God is a god who does not even respect love – in any man. Chapter 14, which universalises the "complaint", applies Job's conclusions to everyone. Given this fact, the negative introduction of the "hope theme", here as elsewhere, simply plays a dramatic role in the unfolding of the *Book of Job*: tension, relieved then tightened a notch, binds the reader more tightly in the coils of tragic identification – almost classic *katharsis*.

That this long speech of 12–14 represents a turning point in the whole drama[15] is seen from the immediate reaction – for once to the point – of Eliphaz in chapter 15. Job's point of view is plain heresy. The "doctrine of God" he has just unfolded is offensive to pious ears, represents rank impiety. The suggestion that one can apply the categories of human reason to God subverts established religion:

Then Eli'phaz the Te'manite answered:
"Should a wise man answer with windy knowledge,
and fill himself with the east wind?

Should he argue in unprofitable talk,
  or in words with which he can do no good?
But you are doing away with the fear of God,
  and hindering meditation before God.
For your iniquity teaches your mouth,
  and you choose the tongue of the crafty.
Your own mouth condemns you, and not I;
  your own lips testify against you."

(15:1–6)

Verse 4 is the real stumbling block as Eliphaz sees it: not an academic argument about injustice or inequity but a theory about God that makes piety – that is, relationship with the divine – impossible. The Hebrew text is forceful:

For you undermine *fear* [of the Lord]
  and render devotion to God impossible.

The word used for "fear" (*yir'a*) represents the fundamental relationship to God *as he is known*, and it is noticeable that the definition of Job, that perfectly religious man of the Prologue, was "one who fears God", using the same term in 1:1 and 1:8. In fact, Terrien notes that the verbal form used here is one that usually applies to the violation of the Covenant, signifying an attitude that renders it empty and futile. In 4:6 Eliphaz himself, in a more conciliatory mood, had spoken sympathetically of his friend's piety in terms of *fear* ("piety") and blameless life. Now he is afraid that Job's argument will destroy his own faith because it represents a denial of traditional theology. It is remarkable how emphasis now falls on vv. 11–13, the intervening vv. 7–10 having been simply *argumentum ad hominem*:[16]

Are the consolations of God too small for you,
  or the word that deals gently with you?
Why does your heart carry you away,
  and why do your eyes flash,
that you turn your spirit against God,
  and let such words go out of your mouth?

(15:11–13)

And in his defence of religion in vv. 14–16 he reiterates *his* theological principle, that man cannot judge God according to rational premises; no man is deserving of justice at God's hands:

> What is man, that he can be clean?
>   Or he that is born of a woman, that he can be righteous?
> Behold, God puts no trust in his holy ones,
>   and the heavens are not clean in his sight;
> how much less one who is abominable and corrupt,
>   a man who drinks iniquity like water!
>
> (15:14–16)

He therefore must simply be accepted, even if this means rationalizing what one sees of his actions in history (vv. 17ff). This is at least a tacit admission that Job's heresy is his use of reason to define the deity. Job's theological adventurism has led him outside the orthodox camp.

Indeed, in the overall development of the debate in the Dialogue one notes with interest how often it is a speech by Eliphaz, reacting to a Jobian *prise-de-position*, that closes a particular movement.[17] Chapter 15 thus shuts the door quite firmly on the protagonist's "meditation on God", and stimulates him to take off on a new lap. Faced with Eliphaz's "declaration of excommunication" Job persists in following reason and arguing the case out to its logical conclusion. Indeed, from chapter 16 on the logic becomes more rigorous and more closely argued as Job draws out in three further speeches the implications of his "heresy". Thus from 16 to 21 the *Book of Job* presents a rational investigation into God, a "triumph of reason over faith", as God's cruelty and injustice are established beyond reasonable doubt.[18]

Developing the rationalist "heresy"

In chapters 16–17, his fourth speech in the Dialogue, Job continues to give reason primacy over faith which, deprived of logic, is simply "windy words", as he impatiently describes the arguments of the friends in 16:3. Loyal speeches mean nothing. God is demonstrably cruel (vv. 6–9) and no longer simply arbitrary: "He has torn me in his wrath and hated me; he has gnashed his teeth at me; my adversary sharpens his eyes against me" (16:9). That means that if the god of Jobian experience is the god of the traditional theologians he is empirically brutal (vv. 11–17) – there are few more savage portraits of the absolute despot in literature than that of God in these verses. He is the implacable enemy of mankind. The accusations made against him by Job occur here in the same form, and using the same images and vocabulary, as are traditionally used in the "Accusation against an Enemy" in the Lament. Murphy sees this section as a Lament, comprising a description of an attack by an enemy (God) and a cry for justice. Like Westermann and others[19] he accepts vv. 19–21, the "witness in heaven", as an "avowal of trust", but even in isolation it is difficult to see how this is possible, since the formal structure of the pericope militates against any such interpretation. Chapter 16 is an attack on God, which largely takes the form of a lament-type accusation against enemies. The enemy is God. It ends with a cry of despair. It is within this immediate context, and the general thrust of the Dialogue to date, that the avowal of a "witness in heaven" must be viewed.

> Even now, behold, my witness is in heaven,
> and he that vouches for me is on high.
>
> (16:19)

This "witness" must be either God himself or some other, presumably lesser, deity.[20] If it is God, Job's only witness is a savage deity who systematically brutalises man. If it is a lesser deity it presupposes a "minor god" created by God himself and therefore one not very likely to be on Job's side when his creator was in opposition. Job expects imminent death (17:1), and the only divinity he knows is malign. What kind of hope is there for him as things stand?[21] What this rather intrusive verse suggests is perhaps a moment of near-schizophrenia as the traditional belief in a caring God vanishes from his mind. God will not even mete out justice, let alone compassion. The friends' wisdom is no wisdom at all (17:10), and the only god the protagonist knows is the very one responsible for a situation that offers no respite but death (17:1.11–16). Job has nothing left but his intellectual integrity.

How solitary his stand is, and how radical, appears in the fact that from now on the arguments of the friends simply peter out – old arguments are disinterred and reiterated, parrot-like. Job now holds the stage alone and opposes the mental construct that is God. Here indeed is Prometheus, but a more cerebral one than Aeschylus presents; chained to an intellectual rock of reason. And like Prometheus he hurls defiance at his God: "Know that God has put me in the wrong, and closed his net about me. Behold, I cry out 'violence!', but I am not answered . . . there is no justice". Stylistically, this major speech of chapter 19 is a remarkably violent reaction – far more so than Job normally indulges in. He is clearly responding to Bildad's traditional theology of act-consequence (18), as he uses the same formula in 19:2 as was used in 18:2 – "How long will you hunt for words . . .?"

> Then Job answered:
> "How long will you torment me,
>   and break me in pieces with words?
> These ten times you have cast reproach upon me;
>   are you not ashamed to wrong me?
> And even if it be true that I have erred,
>   my error remains with myself.
> If indeed you magnify yourselves against me,
>   and make my humilliation an argument against me,
> know then that God has put me in the wrong.
>   and closed his net about me.
> Behold, I cry out, 'Violence!' but I am not answered;
>   I call aloud, but there is no justice.
> He has walled up my way, so that I cannot pass,
>   and he has set darkness upon my paths.
> He has stripped from me my glory,
>   and taken the crown from my head.
> He breaks me down on every side, and I am gone,
>   and my hope has he pulled up like a tree.
> He has kindled his wrath against me,
>   and counts me as his adversary.
> His troops come on together;
>   they have cast up siegeworks against me,

and encamp round about my tent."

(19:1–12)

As a response it is interesting. Since Bildad's thesis was a keystone of theodicy any rejection of it would amount to an attack on the divine order of things, and consequently to a claim that God deforms established order. So Job is proposing the idea that there is no logic to God's attitude towards his creation. He misdirects the cosmic order, which becomes "cosmic disorder" in his hands. In 7:7 he had commented ironically on Ps 8, the great creation poem; here in 19:9 he negates it. In both the psalm and Job 19 "honour" (*kabôd*) and "crown" (*'atarâ*) are used significantly for the relationship between creator and creature. Job's argument is consistent. The creator God destroys his own creation. There is no sharing of responsibility: God is the author of all that befalls Job. And the friends take God's side.

This text of chapter 19 marks a stage of complete alienation from God and from society. It is a strongly sustained accusation that what God is doing to Job is beyond measure or reason. What is important about this chapter is that it shows how the momentum has been maintained since 16:9–14: God himself has become the enemy of man. The formal style of chapter 19 is "Lament against Enemies", the vocabulary and imagery being traditional to that type of literature. Here God is the enemy who has "torn him down" (v. 10). While both Westermann and Murphy agree on this, both suggest that what follows in vv. 23–27 represents a confession of confidence.[22] This does not seem coherent with the structure and style of the chapter. Verses 2–3 are the classic opening accusation of the Lament against Enemies; vv. 7–20 then describe God's savagery towards the protagonist; and vv. 21–24 and 28–29 form a plaintive appeal to the friends that they at least accord him the comfort God refuses. Thus the so-called "affirmation of faith" occurs in between, in vv. 25–27 – notoriously among the most corrupt and ambiguous texts in the book, and most arguments as to meaning tend to be based on conjectural reading.

Most exegetes accept the tradition that here is found an expression of hope, but they differ as to the precise object of that hope: God, or some other "vindicator"?; before or after death? An examination of both text and context would suggest that there is no question at all of "hope", unless the pericope is a redactional interpolation, and there is no evidence of that. What, then, is the scope of these verses?

Meeting the real God: 19:25–27

> But as for me, I know that my vindicator lives [exists?],
>   and afterwards [the Last?] will stand on the dust.
> And after my skin has been destroyed
>   from my flesh I will see God.
> I shall see him for myself, with my own eyes,
>   my heart yearns in my breast.

The translation is gibberish because the text is atrocious. Verse 25a is, quite simply, the only textually clear statement in the pericope, and even that can mean either that "my vindicator (go'el) lives" or that "he exists". The rest is impossible to translate without conjectural reading, since there is not one half-verse without its ambiguities. Verse 25b can be understood adverbially ("afterwards") or substantically ("the one coming after"), but in either case there is a grammatical anomaly. In the same half-verse the phrase "on the dust" is equally disputed: does it mean "on earth" or "upon my grave", before or after death? There are as many answers as there are exegetes. The next two verses, 26 and 27, are best left to crossword addicts – as they stand they are "uncertain, ambiguous and difficult",[23] notoriously a problem for interpreters.

The exegete is left with one half-verse (25a), the immediate context (a lament against an enemy), and the overall thrust of the Dialogue. Even then that half-verse is open to more than one interpretation: is the "vindicator" in question God or someone else? Is he human or non-human? There seems little reason to believe other than that the vindicator of v. 25a is the same person as the "arbiter" of 9:33 and the "witness" of 16:19, *and he is, here as there, God himself.* Nothing has changed. Job, now as then, *knows God exists,* and equally well knows him to be the enemy. He appears in chapter 19 at the centre of what both Murphy and Westermann judge to be an affirmation of faith or confidence, but this section of vv. 23–27 begins with the Hebrew formula "would that . . .", normally used of prayers that are hopeless or impossible. This is not dissimilar to 14:13–22 where a "hope for future reprieve" was no more than a nostalgia, a "would that it were possible" plea. This "hopeless hope" is not new at all. It occurs frequently, often using the same formula (6:2; 14:13; 19:23; 23:3; 29:2; 31:35), but only that it may be dismissed, all in the interests of dramatic tension. If the hope of vindication were real, the change from despair to hope to despair would be very sudden, as Terrien admits, though he claims that the Vindicator cannot be God, arguing convincingly that up to this God has been Job's enemy, and he remains an enemy after this episode. Such a rapid change from persecutor to vindicator back to persecutor would be too sudden and no dramatic development could support it. Pope's argument that the Vindicator, while the same person as 9:33 and 16:19, is not God but a lesser divinity, one who serves the same function as the personal helper-god of Sumerian theology,[24] means little in the context of chapter 19, for if he is not the divinity there can be no effective recourse to him from God's criminal attitude. If such were the case it would presuppose a lesser divinity, presumably created by God himself. Such a one would scarcely be likely to be on Job's side when his creator is not.

Within the movement of the debate Job 19 is in fact a crescendo of violent accusation against God. The protagonist appeals even to the friends for the compassion he cannot expect from God (vv. 21–22). It seems hardly likely that the chapter would now take a different turn and be crowned with an affirmation of hope or faith. Such would be intrusive. Nothing said earlier signals the birth of hope, and the vindicator passage itself does nothing to decrease the momentum or change the direction in which Job's theology has been pointed since chapters 12–14. This is evident from the fact that in *his* response Eliphaz, always the warning-flag for a change of emphasis, is driven to wash his hands completely of Job (22), and for the first time. Thus if the *Book of Job* were truly "Lament genre", and if chapter 19 were an expression of hope, then the highpoint would have to be this "Vindicator" speech, and it is this that would be followed by the Theophany. But the thought not only carries on, it actually develops after this. And the real development of an argument against God comes *after* chapter 22, in several Jobian speeches. The Theophany is not an answer to Job's need, or to his prayer; *it is an answer to his logic*, which has yet some way to go. The "vindicator theme" of this chapter 19 does no more than underline the ghastly helplessness of Job's position. It is a sharp exclamation of pain wrung from man by a savage God, to be dropped immediately as reason gains ascendency. Quite simply – God is no use as a vindicator. And this awareness is meant to point the inevitable question: "what sort of God are we talking about?"

Mounting the attack against God

For the second time Zophar sees the way Job's logic is headed:

> Zophar the Naamathite spoke, and said:
> "Therefore my troubled mind forces me to answer
>   because I am so deeply disturbed.
> I hear a statement that dishonours me,
>   and my spirit of understanding prompts me to reply."
> (20:1–3)

In vv. 2–3 he recognizes Job's intransigence ("a statement that dishonours me") – he is "troubled in mind" because of what he has *just* heard; "therefore" signals a situation of immediate response, and this is strange for Zophar, whose usual style of debate is acrimonious rather than responsive. Also, the word "godless" in v. 5 is carefully chosen to describe Job: "The triumph of the wicked

70

is brief, and the joy of the *godless* does not last". Like Eliphaz in chapter 15, Zophar can recognize heresy when he hears it. And he is responding to the speech of chapter 19.

Job's answer in chapter 21 is basically the same as his last response to Zophar (chapter 12), though the style is suitably changed. Chapter 21 is a wisdom poem. Using the argument from experience as they themselves have often enough done (4:7f; 5:1f; 8:8f; 15:17f; 18:5f; 20:4f), Job shows how the wicked prosper – that is the fact. Zophar's argument is no more than a far too facile repetition of traditional theodicy, blind to facts. God's trustworthiness cannot be proved, either from experience or from reason, for he does not send sure retribution in this life.

> Why do the wicked live,
>   reach old age, and grow mighty in power?
> Their children are established in their presence,
>   and their offspring before their eyes.
> Their houses are safe from fear,
>   and no rod of God is upon them.
> Their bull breeds without fail;
>   their cow calves, and does not cast her calf.
> They send forth their little ones like a flock,
>   and their children dance.
> They sing to the tambourine and the lyre,
>   and rejoice to the sound of the pipe.
> They spend their days in prosperity,
>   and in peace they go down to Sheol.
> They say to God, "Depart from us!
>   We do not desire the knowledge of thy ways.
> What is the Almighty, that we should serve him?
>   And what profit do we get if we pray to him?"
> Behold, is not their prosperity in their hand?
>   The counsel of the wicked is far from me.
>
> (21:7–16)

This may be a strong statement for a theologian but Job, the bit firmly between his teeth, goes further. *God gives prosperity to the wicked* – a logical development from his last response to the same interlocutor where it was seen that God misuses his omnipotence. The wicked ignore him yet he rewards them,[25] thus showing that there is no necessary connection between faith and prosperity, righteousness and reward. What is most obvious in these verses is the fact that the description of the lot of the wicked is very much the same as the traditional picture of the righteous. Thus it is not so much that Job is presenting a reversal of traditional theology (the wicked prosper) as it is a rejection of God's ordering of the cosmos. This means that there is no logic to his ways, as vv. 17–33 now show:

> How often is it that the lamp of the wicked is put out?
>> That their calamity comes upon them?
>> That God distributes pains in his anger?
> That they are like straw before the wind,
>> and like chaff that the storm carries away?
> You say, "God stores up their iniquity for their sons."
>> Let him recompense it to themselves, that they may know it.
> Let their own eyes see their destruction,
>> and let them drink of the wrath of the Almighty.
> For what do they care for their houses after them,
>> when the number of their months is cut off?
> Will any teach God knowledge,
>> seeing that he judges those that are on high?
> One dies in full prosperity,
>> being wholly at ease and secure,
> his body full of fat
>> and the marrow of his bones moist.
> Another dies in bitterness of soul,
>> never having tasted of good.
> They lie down alike in the dust,
>> and the worms cover them.
> Behold, I know your thoughts,
>> and your schemes to wrong me.
> For you say, "Where is the house of the prince?
>> Where is the tent in which the wicked dwelt?"
> Have you not asked those who travel the roads,
>> and do you not accept their testimony
> that the wicked man is spared in the day of calamity,
>> that he is rescued in the day of wrath?
> Who declares his way to his face,
>> and who requites him for what he has done?
> When he is borne to the grave,

watch is kept over his tomb.
The clods of the valley are sweet to him;
    all men follow after him,
    and those who go before him are innumerable.

It is not simply that the just suffer and the wicked prosper, but that one cannot *rely* on it either way. It is also noticeable that both sections of this chapter, that is vv. 7–16 and vv. 17–33, *begin with a question*. Job is probing the limits of the tradition: in the light of experience, what is the wise man to think? Certainly, he must not simply accept the ready-made theories of professional theologians – life shows a different pattern. This brand of thinking opens the door to a more widely based and more universal understanding of truth.

It is at this point that Eliphaz, in his reply of chapter 22, closes the friends' involvement in the debate. He establishes the gap between man and God, strengthening the point he made before in 15:14f, and then goes for the jugular: God is transcendent; therefore what man does affects him not at all.

> Then Eliphaz the Temanite answered:
> "Can a man be profitable to God?
>   Surely he who is wise is profitable to himself.
> Is it any pleasure to the Almighty if you are righteous,
>   or is it gain to him if you make your ways blameless?
> Is it for your fear of him that he reproves you,
>   and enters into judgment with you?
> Is not your wickedness great?
>   There is no end to your iniquities.

(22:1–5)

It must therefore be clear that if man suffers he has deserved it; he alone profits from his good deeds, and so he suffers the effects of his wickedness. Thus, arguing backwards from conclusion (based on dogma) to principle, Eliphaz attributes moral turpitude to Job. His listing of examples (vv. 6ff) is simply a text-book exercise – they all derive from traditional ethics. He can think of nothing else to say – hostage as he is to his own dogma – so with this speech he simply closes the door to further debate.[26] Dialogue is ended; from now on Job presses his attack directly on God against the background noise of the second and third friends' angry and inarticulate interjections. Yet he can take as his starting point one of the ideas proposed by Eliphaz, though not in the way the latter understood it: God *is* beyond answerability to man. The protagonist sees evidence of this in his capriciousness and his cruelty: he can do as he wishes, man has no way of retaliating. And so Job launches into a quasi-philosophical dissertation on the nature of God seen in the way man's sphere of existence intersects with God's prepotence.

Bringing God to trial

Chapters 23:1–24:12 form the last identifiable speech in this first part of the *Book of Job*. Everything that comes after is so jumbled that no universally acceptable attribution of speeches can be offered. However, ignoring the words of both Bildad and Zophar, and concentrating on what can with some certitude be attributed to Job, a coherent picture emerges of God – as he appears to human reason. As MacKenzie points out[27], chapters 23–24 represent "Job's personal reflections and his search for God". And what is immediately obvious is the fact that God is an aloof divinity whom one cannot reach. This is reminiscent of the Kafka novel, *The Trial*, where the protagonist, Joseph K, is arrested for an unspecified crime. He searches out the judge, believing that if he can reach him all will be resolved. Finally he arrives at a closed door. The judge is within – one sees the light shine beneath the door – but he will not come out and Joseph K cannot go in to him.[28] This whole Kafkaesque process of searching for a "trial" in which the two antagonists, man and God, would finally meet and one of the two find justification, is highlighted from the very beginning by the repetition of the by now familiar formula "would that . . ." in v. 3:

> *Would that* I knew where I could find him . . .
> I would lay my case before him.

God exists: one knows he is there behind a closed door, but Job also knows he will never get him to come to judgement. "Would that . . ." says it all. And as the protagonist pushes out further and further from the safe shore of traditional belief in a just and compassionate God he becomes progressively more independent of accepted dogma. As if the friends no longer existed Job now broods on the God of his own experience, whom he now sees as one who will never grant the trial the vindication he desires nor enter the tribunal where Job could state his case.

This underlines the futility of man's search for God. In spite of his need for encounter, however, he has sufficient intellectual integrity not to postulate a "convenient divinity" suited to his own needs. He has no claim on the divinity – does the divinity have any claim on him? Even an ethical one? What God wants he does, and this is frightening, for it reveals a divinity who is unaccountable and unknowable, a creator who allows his world to drift. So, reasonably enough, men become criminal anarchists carrying on as if he did not exist, and he seems to tolerate this attitude!

> Men remove landmarks;
>> they seize flocks and pasture them.
> They drive away the ass of the fatherless;
>> they take the widow's ox for a pledge.
> They thrust the poor off the road;
>> the poor of the earth all hide themselves.
> From out of the city the dying groan,
>> and the soul of the wounded cries for help;
>> yet God pays no attention to their prayer.

(24:2–4.12)

This speech passes from a sense of personal injustice to one of social injustice: a world to which God is blind and deaf. God has done more than "destroy Job's hope" – he has destroyed the cosmic order. This is the last word. God remains beyond human comprehension, and in 26–27 Job simply holds fast to his new "theology", and to his intellectual integrity – before *God* as well as before men.

1. "No one is righteous before God" is perhaps a hebraicization of a common Mesopotamian teaching. See the "Babylonian Theodicy", in W.G. Lamber, *Babylonian Wisdom Literature*, Oxford, 1960, 63–91, and S.N. Kramer, "Man and his God. A Sumerian variation of the 'Job' Motif", in *VIS* 3(1955), 170–182.

2. It is noticeable that from 4:19 to 5:17 it develops from an implicit tradition to an explicit credo. See Wiser, *Das Buch Hiob*, 14; MacKenzie, in *JBC*, 517 and Habel, *Book of Job*, 33.

3. See R.E. Murphy, *Forms of Old Testament Literature*, 26; G. Fohrer, *Das Buch Hiob*, Gütersloh, 1963, 186 and E. Dhorme, *A Commentary on the Book of Job*, London, 1967, xxxviii.

4. C. Westermann, *Structure of the Book of Job*, 53, observes: "The accusation against God in chaps. 9–10 strikes one as a high point that is hard to surpass. The accusation only intimated in chap. 3 is so intensified through chaps. 9–10 that one has to ask how the continuance of this theme in chaps. 12–14 is to be understood."

5. Dhorme, *op. cit.*, xxxix, holds that Job seems to have ignored Bildad so as to answer Eliphaz, but more probably Bildad's argument has started a train of thought that sends Job back to Eliphaz – really the only opposing theological argument – and from there on to new theological developments.

6. L. Lévèque, *Job et son Dieu. Essai d'exégèse et de théologie biblique*, Paris, 1970, 355, holds that the "pecadilloes" for which Job is punished could not possibly merit such a violent response from God – disproportionate – so it must come from a *deliberate desire* to hurt. The same author holds, p.354, that in traditional texts that deal with "God's anger" there is always a question of a sanction for infringement of his law, but not in *Job*.

7. See L. Alonso Schökel & J.L. Sicre Diaz, *Job*, 181; Pope, *Job*, 78. This was already hinted at, as M. Dahood observes in "Some Northwest-Semitic words in Job", in *Bib* 38(1957), 311f, where he reads 9:20 as "if I am innocent he would declare me guilty", reading *pa* (Ugaritic "and, for, then") in place of the Hebrew *pî*, a reading confirmed by 9:22. As A. Camus observes, "either man is a captive being, in which case God is responsible for evil; or man is responsible, in which case God is not omnipotent": *Le Mythe de Sisyphe*, Paris, 1942, 79.

8. Murphy, *Forms*, 27, sees chap. 9:25–10:1a as a speech addressed by Job to himself, and 10:1ab–22 as a speech addressed to God. See also Pope, *Job*, xvi.

9. As Dhorme, *op. cit.*, cxxxvi, thinks: "a satire attacking the moralists who think that they alone are the inheritors of sound doctrine." See also J.G. Williams, " 'You have not spoken truth of Me'. Mystery and Irony in Job", in *ZAW* 83(1971), 236. Murphy, *Forms*, 29. See also Westermann, *Structure*, 53, who notes how the style breaks in chap. 13.

11. In this *mashal* which is Job's "oath of clearance", he shows how he has been compassionate towards the weak beyond what the law demanded. See also G. Fohrer, "The Righteous Man in Job 31", in *Essays in Old Testament Ethics* (ed. J.L. Crenshaw & J.T. Willis), New York, 1974, 8.

12. See Westermann, "The Two faces of Job", in *Concilium* 160(1983), 18.

13. For example, Terrien, *Job*, 123, speaks of the restoration of the relationship of mutual love, and H.H. Rowley, *Job*, 20f, holds for the loving presence of God.

14. Also an echo of 3:17–18:22. Pope, *op. cit.*, xvi: "There is no hope in the

hereafter (xiv 7–12). If only there were such a hope, he would wait his turn (xiv 13–15). But the only prospect is extinction (xiv 18–22)." See also MacKenzie, in *JBC*, 520.

15. Westermann, *Structure*, 54. See Pope, *op. cit.*, 108: "Eliphaz's second speech opens the second cycle. He is much less courteous and less conciliatory than in his previous speech. He now accuses Job of mouthing a lot of hot air and nonsense. He charges him with subversion of piety . . . Whereas Eliphaz regarded Job at first as an essentially pious man only temporarily and lightly chastised by God, he now sees him as a hardened sinner and rebel against God."

16. Terrien, *Job*, 126. Also, the "tongue of the crafty", using the word *'arûmîm*, in 15:5. Eliphaz may be thinking of the "serpent" in Gen. 3, according to Terrien. If he is, the "first man" of v. 7 may lead to an identification with Adam, the motif of the universal "Adam" who usurps his freedom to choose to judge the divinity. See D.J.A. Clines, "The Arguments of Job's Three Friends", in *Art and Meaning: Rhetoric in Biblical Literature* (JSOTS 19), Sheffield, 1982, 199–214; though this author would see this as Eliphaz rebuking Job for letting his tongue run away with him: in the light of vv. 14–34 "an elaborate sketch of the kind of person Job is *not*, but is in danger of becoming." Certainly, vv. 7–9, a wisdom argument in primary colours, suggest that Job is making a claim (similar to that of Wisdom personified in Prov 8 and Wis 7–9) that he is immediately close to the divine mind. Clearly Eliphaz sees that it is the concept of God that is in question.

17. Chapters 4–5 are a reaction to chapter 3 and lay the foundation for Job's argument of commensurate suffering and his subsequent meditation on God. Similarly, chapter 15 is a reaction against this, just as 22 is a reaction against the whole argument to date.

18. For Dhorme, *op. cit.*, XLIV, here in the second cycle "the rigour of the logic is more marked than anywhere else in the poetic section." The two theses are presented with a skill that normally surpasses that of orientals: the righteous are punished, the wicked are as happy as anyone can be. There is something of the logic of Qohelet in this Jobian position. In chapters 16–21 Job seems to be responding more coherently to the cumulative argument of the friends than heretofore: 16–17 responds (word for word, 16:4–6) to Eliphaz (15); 19 is an answer to Bildad (18 and 8); 21 responds to Zophar's repeated argument (12 and 20). Perhaps Job is "tying up" the debate before he turns definitively to his real adversary, God, in 23–24.

19. Westermann, *op. cit.*, 45; Murphy, *op. cit.*, 31. See also N.C. Habel, *The Book of Job*, 267, and Weiser, *op. cit.*, 126.

20. Pope, *op. cit.*, LXXI, suggests it reflects a Mesopotamian idea of a "personal god whose function it was to look after his client's interest and plead his cause in the divine assembly." See also, on both sides of the argument, S. Kramer, "Man and his God", and Terrien, *Job*, 131f. See also J.G. Williams, "You have not spoken truth of Me", 243.

21. *Loc. cit.*, "At times Job seems certain of his own death before vindication, if vindicated he might be. Here he cries out in a lament of the innocent dead . . . Job's outcry is usually construed as a note of hope. But what kind of hope! His blood on the earth (see Gen 4:10ff) indicates that he anticipates his death and now hopes for a vindication of his name, though he be dead."

22. As in 16:9–14 so here God himself has become the enemy – accusations about him are made in the form, traditional images and vocabulary of the lament about enemies. "Substantively these passages belong in the context of accusation against God, and this is how they are spoken . . .", Wester-

mann, *Structure*, 45. He adds that we *now* find an avowal of trust. See also Murphy, *op. cit.*, 33.

23. S.R. Driver & G.B. Gray, *The Book of Job* (ICC), 128. Dhorme, *op. cit.*, 284; Rowley, *op. cit.*, 139; Pope, *op. cit.*, 134, and many others.
24. Terrien, *Job*, 150f; Pope, *op. cit.*, 135. It is interesting to note that a similar formula is used, which may be the inspiration behind Job 19:25: "I know that triumphant Baal lives . . .", in J.B. Pritchard, *Ancient Near Eastern Texts relating to the Old Testament*, Princeton, 1969, 140. See also Williams, "You have not spoken truth of Me", 244.
25. "The happiness of men without God", is the way MacKenzie describes it in *JBC*, 524.
26. Dhorme, *op. cit.*, xlv. Indeed, Terrien suggests that he is a theologian of salvation through works, *op. cit.*, 170. According to Dhorme the interlocutors do not address each other in this cycle, *op. cit.*, xlvii.
27. MacKenzie, in *JBC*, 525.
28. F. Kafka, *Der Prozess*, Munich, 1925. A similar theme is found in much of Kafka's work, such as *The Castle*.

Chapter 5

What has the dialogue achieved?

What emerges from a reading of Job 3–31 is the perception that two things have disturbed the friends and characterize the author's thinking: Job is propounding a strange "theology of God", and he has adopted a new way of "making theology" by arguing from experience rather than tradition. The whole process poses a major problem: if the basis of morality be overturned can theology survive? If the relationship between man and his God cannot be clearly delineated, according to recognizable norms of reciprocal "laws", *can God be known at all?*[1] Certainly, to those involved in the actual dialogue, Job has a distinguishable theology of God that is considered heretical.

What can one know about God?

The sapiential tradition in fact allowed the possibility of speaking about God a-theistically, as it were, in that it presents a balanced relationship, an act-consequence correlation: it presents God as one who preserves what he has created, but without necessarily naming him. Job approaches the problem from the opposite direction: for him the Creator is *not* a preserver of what he has created, and he is named. God is an anarchist, and man is no more than a creature arbitrarily cast into a lawless world. Israel, like her neighbours, was intellectually and theologically tied to a tradition of "design", an ordered cosmos created by God, ruled by him according to perceptible laws by which man must act so as to be "human", an integral part of a harmonious whole. But experience has, for Job, proved this false. In chapters 4–14 the contrast between God the creator and God the destroyer of his own creation is brought out forcefully. This destructiveness of God is not simply addressed to the wicked, it embraces the righteous, remaining thus mysterious and incomprehensible. It quite simply is not "deserved" – it does not conform to any perceptible "order". It is ethically without significance. This is not the point of view of the friends. Already in chapter 5 Eliphaz holds to the tradition that God's reversal of creation affects only the wicked – therefore God is logical. But to Job he is a-logical[2], and so the rationalist concludes that God is blind and arbitrary. They are all – friends and protagonist alike – convinced that God is ultimately responsible for man's actual condition, and that one can conclude *something* thereby. This is basic. For the friends human suffering is punitive or corrective – it is theologically immaterial which, since both fit the theological premises. Job cannot see any correspondence of act and consequence (16:12; 27:2–6), and his request that he might *know* finds no hearing – as it should if the Lament-form reflected the *Sitz-im-Leben* of the drama. The friends are particularly interested in the fate of the ungodly, not the godly. They *presume* Job is ungodly in some sense because God does not allot his condition to someone righteous: *presumptio theologica.* But the protagonist, like the reader, in interested in the fate of the godly, for he is proceeding from empirical data – the experience of unmerited suffering: *experience universalized*. Yet it is not the existence of senseless suffering that is tragic, but the existence of a "just God" responsible for this state of affairs. If "integrity" does mean for the Hebrew that his relationship to the environment is one of *shalom*, as Terrien holds[3], then the protagonist of the Dialogue is not integrated as was the Job of the Prologue, or even of the Theophany. And it is precisely this character, revealed in chapters 4–27, that dominates the whole *Book of Job*: a dramatic protagonist searching for the intellectual and rational basis of the essential "I-thou" relationship that is theology. For if God exists there must also exist certain objective values, that is, values outside of man's own "self". This underlines the difference between Job and the friends. For them, such values exist. But that is the danger. If God exists, then the existence of objective values dispenses man from his responsibility of choice. He would be able to rest on the comfortable cushion of ready-made certitudes and no longer know the anxiety that is the mark of the free man.[4]

From the standpoint of the reader of the book, the profit lies in the fact that for Job such values do *not* exist. In this fable God is a creator who destroys his creation, a divinity who reverses his own design. And this raises the problem of relationship. What bond can there be between such a God and his creature? Can there be *any* human relationship with Caliban? This is the ground of the debate. If justice – man's or God's – were the argument then Eliphaz's first speech would have solved it: no man is righteous before God; he alone makes the ground-rules (4–5; 15; 25).[5] Job also knows this (9). The real question is: *what kind of a God* is it that, given man's "normal lack of righteousness" (i.e. his humanity) will mete out suffering and well-being arbitrarily? What norms is he using? What is his nature? That which in *Psalms* is a belief in God becomes in *Job* an enquiry into God, and belief in a relationship with him has become a critique of that relationship.

God exists for an individual only if that individual can think of him and relate to him, and the *way* one thinks of God depends on the relationship. Does one experience him as a God of love? – then a God of love he is, as for Eliphaz in 22:23–26: "If you return to the Almighty and humble yourself, if you remove unrighteousness far from your tents . . . then you will delight yourself in the Almighty, and lift up your face to God". Does another experience him as a judge? – then for *that* individual he *is* a judge, as he is for the more prosaic Bildad in 8:3–6: "If your children have sinned against him, he has delivered them into the power of their transgression . . . But if you are pure and upright, surely then he will rouse himself for you and reward you with a rightful habitation". The brutal fact is that God exists only to the extent that one thinks of him and *only as one perceives him*. So the crucial question is: on the basis of which particular mode of perception or mental image of him does one project him? On the basis of an inherited tradition that sees him primarily as a creator God who established a well-ordered cosmos and governs it in justice? Or on the basis of an experience of disorder, injustice and absurdity that contradicts that tradition? Already by the end of the first fourteen chapters the principle has been established that what has been actually experienced cannot be refuted on the basis of an inherited theory alone. One is part of reality, the other pertains to the realm of speculation. Eliphaz and Job are agreed on one thing:[6] to both, God is a judge, transcendent and omnipotent. But their moral assessment differs: to Eliphaz he is just and even merciful; to Job he is arbitrary and intermittently cruel. He is a God who can will evil on people – and therefore he is not a "moral" God in any identifiable sense. And he should be! Job's anger comes from a clearly ethical vision of the divinity: suffering makes sense if it responds to justice; if it does not fit into any just pattern it is an obscenity. For this reason – because to him "God" can only mean a god of justice – Job must revolt against the absurdity created by a "just God", that is, "a suffering just man".

Rethinking the proposition "God"

Since the putative "divine order" has failed to withstand the test of experience man must go his own way and discover his own verities. The *Book of Job* begins this enquiry with a laboratory situation: a perfectly just man. If, then, God is a just judge a certain balance of deed-consequence is to be expected. Human conduct sets up a chain-reaction that begins with man and returns to him: his integrity will redound to his own *shalom*[7]; Job is a man of integrity but it redounds to alienation. Therefore there is no ethical principle that ties man to God.

. . . you helped me
Establish once for all the principle
There's no connection man can reason out
Between his just deserts and what he gets.
(Robert Frost, A Masque of Reason)

The key is not so much the "justice of man, injustice of God" as it is the erosion of the intellectual basis for "faith". Man has been given a mind to use, and the fundamental attitude of the sapiential writers was the use of experience as a norm of reality. The resultant dialectic of experience and reason may be imperfect, but it must be valid! That is why the "cry for justice" of Job 16:18 is a deliberate formula: a rudimentary appeal for the most basic legal justice, which is not to be *proved* innocent but to have it explained beyond reasonable doubt. When Job "cries out" $(z'q)$ in the forensic scenes he is not complaining about unjust suffering – for suffering is neither just nor unjust. He has already recognized that God's deeds are not subject to man's laws and so he acknowledges the "divine freedom to root justice where he pleases".[8] His "cry" is for the loss of the wisdom norm of experience allied to reason. Perhaps it could be said that what most aggravates the friends (especially from chapter 8 on) is the protagonist's stubborn refusal to submit his "argument from experience" to their "faith".

But Job has hit on a crucial truth of existence. It is essential to be able to feel that, in both religious and social life, one is in accord with an ultimate cosmic design. That was Dante's vision. It was not evident to the poet of *Job*. Chapter 9:32 clearly acknowledges the fact that God is not bound to act in any given way – he cannot be reduced to being the subject of a moral order or rational idea, so there can be no question of an umpire between the divinity and man. But man himself is a judge – he must be or he abdicates his whole tradition of learning. This is the route undertaken by Job. His enquiry into God is an analysis of the absurd, since existentialism's basic concern is a concern with ethics[9] and God is unethical. The result is an intellectual struggle to find a point of anchorage in the midst of a crisis that defies reason. For the theist the starting point is God, and therefore the "problem" is a personal question of the relationship between man and his concept of God. Job has discovered a god who is Lord of Absurdity. Given this fact the first ethical reaction is, in existentialist terms[10], an attitude of revolt, a rejection of traditional "solutions" and evasions. This revolt begins by being theistic; it accepts God but is directed against a state of affairs. In time it becomes a-theistic, because it assigns effects to causes and finds God guilty – thereby subjecting God as well as world to human judgement. This is necessary. The fact is, as Unamuno pointed out in the *Tragic Sense of Life*, that those who believe in God and yet have no passion in their hearts or anguish in their minds – no uncertainty, no doubt, no element of despair – believe not in God but in a god-idea. This was the attitude of both protagonist and friends before the onset of suffering and of the alienation that results from the interrogation of suffering. Since this latter is the ultimate reality to Job the question that faces the reader of the book is: what end does human suffering serve?[11] Either events in the human sphere are explainable by reference to a "divine order" or everything remains absurd. At this level Job is voicing the artist's view rather than the theologian's, a fact the friends fail to appreciate. The only religion that is intellectually tenable is one that acknowledges absurdity. The alternative is a religion in which everything is rational (that of the friends), and this means a religion in which God is understandable.

The artist's contribution to theological method

Thus the function of the Dialogue is to offset the concept of a comprehensible god by one that presents the numinous, for this is the only god that experience can suggest.[12] It is in fact a central perception of classical Judaism that every man knows there is the ineffable, that there is more than what he comprehends.[13] Job 3–31 is an effort at examining, to the limit of human intelligence, this mystery. And the author begins with the datum of experience that was

84

numinous: the combined feeling of attraction and aw[...]

most evident to his contemporaries: God's extraordinary arbitrariness. It is to this cause that Job has traced his own absurd condition. In this way the vision of disorder does more than serve as a critique of the friends' attitudes; it leads directly to an appreciation of the mystery of God. In an almost paradoxical way, to Judaism "mystery" is more real than "comprehension". The emphasis for much of the Old Testament is on the "knowability" of God, but to the thinker more often than not man is caught up in an existence he can apprehend but not comprehend. Perhaps this is why the Talmud presents the book as a *mashal*. If the theologian loses sight of this fact, he loses sight of the reality of a creator god. It is important to note how the point habitually made by the creation psalms, and by the Theophany later on in *Job*, is not the beauty of nature but its sublime aspects, which forces man to re-think the proposition "God".[14]

In a sense, it might be taken that the function served by the Dialogue of Job 3–31 is to illustrate the inadequacy of the theological method and the need for art. To some extent the doctrine of act-consequence had become a complacent theology. Such inevitably breeds a need to bring people back to a clearer understanding of the human condition than theology serves; to make them perceive through the medium of art that the individual stands as a finitude in the midst of an infinite cosmos to which he simultaneously belongs and is alien.[15] Job's mind has made him master of the world, but tradition reminds him of his creaturely nature. The dramatic structure of the first part of the "debate" – that with a human adversary – woos the reader away from the self-satisfaction that arises from firmly established theological categories of "justice" and "order" and brings him face to face with reality. What concerns the author in these chapters is the credibility of a God "created" by a theological tradition. Suffering itself, even when undeserved, can be understood – attributed to a cause – it is God who cannot.

Thus, contrary to what Westermann holds[16], the certainty of Job lies not in trust in God, but solely in the power of the human mind to query the "god-idea". Even on grounds of dramatic unity trust in the God of the tradition is impossible as an ingredient in Job 4–27. This is a work of contestation and as such has no place for gentlemanly compromise. Had Prometheus, even for a moment, conceded anything to Zeus then Aeschylus would not have had a drama at all. For the only "dramatic movement" in either play lies in the intransigence of the dialogue. The words *are* the play, and they must be violent and unyielding to carry the play. Only as such do they represent man's rage in the face of God's omnipotence. Man cannot simply back down before the unreason of the divine attitude if he is to maintain his human dignity. This is exemplified by the "bourgeois Irish Catholics" of Beckett's plays who "use their illusory certainties to protect themselves from ever having to face the disturbing mysteries that the hero sets out to explore".[17] It is a like case with Job and his friends – one reason, perhaps, why the latter disappear from the scene after chapter 27: in the argument with God that constitutes the second "panel" of the *Book of Job* (the Theophany of 38–42) it is the divine point of view, and the theologian's method, that is pressed and no longer human rebellion and the artist's method. Man's greatness lies in his awareness of the value of rebellion, as Camus observes; rebellion not so much against the terms in which existence is given, as against the submissiveness and the unthinking acceptance that allows these terms to determine reality. On his own showing, God's arbitrary attitude to creation, as perceived by Job, seems to demand such a submission. But every thinking person, everyone who lives by the mind, must have a certain degree of scepticism regarding traditional ideas and beliefs that seem to contradict reality as it is actually experienced, and must on occasion renounce those received ideas if they make no sense. This denial of unsubstantiated "theory about God and his control of creation" may eventually lead to a "knowledge of God" that transcends "received faith".[18]

In chapter 4 the Jobian poet began with conventional theology; in chapters 5–27 he shows its inadequacy in the light of what can be experienced – man's actual situation. From that point he is forced to carry on and interrogate that which we call "God". In doing so he judges that God.[19] This attitude is born of a desire to reach beyond the world and touch the transcendent, at least with the mind, for the word "God" has meaning only to the extent that the mind grasps it.[20] One must first experience the pain of contradiction, of having one's certainties about God shattered, before he can make a personally valid decision about transcendence.[21] The reason is that the signs pointing to the absolute are ambiguous, and therefore obscure. The philosophically complacent Job of the Prologue had accepted a view of God that could not stand the test of experience.[22] Since, given his circumstances, he could not deny the *existence* of God he is forced to question a particular way of seeing him, or rather "a god who is conceived in a certain way"[23], and he is forced to use the only instrument left to him – his mind. In his commentary Pope asks: "why the devilish sadistic experiment to see if [Job] had a breaking point?" Perhaps because the Prologue sets the stage for what is going to be an enquiry into *the sort of God who could push man to a breaking point*. The strange character of God is what dominates the Prologue – a "god" as he appears to many people: aloof, inscrutable, indulging in a private game of chess with a human pawn. How can one take seriously the concept of a relationship with such a god – one who has abandoned his own "truth" and so contradicts theology? Innocent – or even disproportionate – suffering must set a question-mark to the whole religious tradition, for the unjust God of experience is also the God of faith.[24] As Murphy observes, the Prologue sets the stage of Job's reaction by presenting "the underside of God", foreshadowed in 2:3 and developed by the protagonist in chapters 7:9 and 12. What might be called the "Caliban effect" is dramatically signalled in the first two chapters and the alert reader of the subsequent Dialogue is ready for its inevitable re-appearance as the play proceeds. In chapter 21 this has become a category for evaluating the tradition: if there be wicked who flourish why should there not equally be righteous who suffer? Once this point is established a principle appears: that righteousness has nothing to do with retribution; and a conclusion is inevitable: what happens in life comes without discrimation to good and bad, and so suffering or prosperity must be viewed independently of theodicy. Therefore God's government of the world is not in question: *his nature as God is*! In this regard 24:12 is perhaps the strongest statement in the book and it furnishes a key to the poet's purpose:

> The groans of the dying rise up in the city;
> the wounded cry out for help.
> *But God charges no one with wrongdoing.*

That says more about God than about right or wrong.

The God of reason

At the end of the Dialogue one is left with a God who has no rules, who defines "justice" in a different way, who is wider in his dispositions than reason can cope with. Certainly the movement of the drama that ends with chapter 31 turns the reader's mind from the more obvious theological concerns with theodicy or ethics to an awareness of God as he is: transcendent, incomprehensible, "irreducible to the schematic formulae" of man's traditional way of thinking about the divine, as a contemporary exegete has shown.[25] Many authors hold that Job discovers the holiness or the love of God, but it is difficult to see where this happens, at least in the Dialogue. He is not described by the protagonist as loving, and while two important texts do speak of man loving God the first (22:26) is spoken by Eliphaz and the second (27:10) is a savage refutation on the lips of Job. Love plays no positive role in the book. What Job *does* rise to, at critical points in the drama, is an insight into the nature of God: "he is not a man as I am . . ." (9:32), "he does not see things from man's point of view" (10:4). The God discovered by the Dialogue is the "totally other", not containable by the human mind. So concepts such as "loving", "good" or even more basic "just" simply do not apply.

This is the crucial point to the author. Man's primal drive

88

is to know, but of its nature the quest for knowledge is limited. This fact in itself becomes a witness to God's nature – he cannot be known in any adequate sense.

In what, then, lies the value of the first part of the *Book of Job*, the poetic Dialogue? Not the discovery of God, he has been perceived as arbitrary by other biblical writers and Job finds nothing new in that aspect of the divinity; nor even the perception that he cannot be discovered, for that also is a truism to the thinker.[26] Perhaps what is new is the intellectual process itself, the path Job took to reach his conclusions: the process of pure reason. At the end of the Dialogue one thing is certain[27]: it is Job alone who has come out of the conflict with an enhanced dignity. They drove blind Oedipus from Thebes, but he remains the tragic hero, for ultimately man can only be ennobled by the capriciousness of God.

NOTES

1. Absolutely shattering, for the "knowability" of God is a cornerstone of Torah as of prophetic religion.
2. As he was to Zophar in chapter 11, though Zophar draws a different conclusion.
3. Terrien, *Job*, 38.
4. This idea is developed in C. Moeller, *Littérature du XX siècle et christianisme, II: La Foi en Jésus-Christ*, Tournai, 1967, 88f, speaking of *The Brothers Karamazov*.
5. Chapter 25 is attributed to Bildad, but the style and formulation is much closer to that of Eliphaz, and it is quite likely that this chapter is a response to Eliphaz. See M.P. Reddy, "The Book of Job – a Reconstruction", in *ZAW* 90(1978), 74.
6. See an interesting presentation by B. Vawter, *Job and Jonah. Questioning the Hidden God*, New York, 1983, 60–62.
7. At this level God is concerned only to the extent that he places this "law" in creation. See P. Ricoeur, *The Symbolism of Evil*.
8. See a hint of this, though used as a different argument, in A.M. Dubarle, *Les Sages d'Israel*, Paris, 1946, 75.
9. R.Y. Hathorn, *Tragedy, Myth and Mystery*, Bloomington, 1966, 80. Also W. Vischer, "God's Truth and Man's Lie. A Study of the Message of the Book of Job", in *Int* 15(1961), 139.
10. For Camus "the first ethical consequence of the absurd is an attitude of perpetual revolt", which is in fact "a continuously defiant rejection of all suggested solutions and evasions since these cannot, *in the nature of things*, be successful or satisfactory": J. Cruickshank, *Albert Camus and the Literature of Revolt*, Oxford, 1970, 70.

11. In his epigraph to *The Lawless Roads* Graham Greene speaks of the human disorders that are evident in life, seeing them as a form of suffering. That suffering only becomes meaningful if it leads to scepticism about God: R. Sharrock, *Saints, Sinners and Comedians. The Novels of Graham Green*, London, 1984, 183.

12. Ravasi, *Giobbe*, 103, makes a point that suffering is a way to illuminate or criticize the various theologies of faith, of retribution, of the reality of being a creature, of the mystery of the divine. It serves as a kind of sounding board.

13. This idea is found in the theological writings of modern Judaism as well, as for example A. Heschel, *Between God and Man. An Interpretation of Judaism*, New York, 1965, 46f.

14. This, perhaps, is the key to the "second panel" of the diptych that is formed by the Yahweh Speeches: God as he sees himself – the second of the two poles that supply the reader with the key to interpretation of the *Book of Job*.

15. Hathorn, *Tragedy, Myth and Mystery*, 29.

16. C. Westermann, "The Two Faces of Job", in *Concilium* 169(1983), 21.

17. E. Webb, *The Plays of Samuel Beckett*, London, 1972, 57.

18. T.S. Eliot, *Essays Ancient and Modern*, London, 1936, 150f: "Every man who thinks and lives by thought must have his own scepticism, that which stops at the question, that which ends in denial, and that which leads to faith and which is somehow integrated in the faith which transcends it . . ."

19. S. Terrien, *The Elusive Presence. The Heart of Biblical Theology*, San Francisco, 1983, 362, says that "the poet found a way to go beyond the scandal of inexplicable pain and to probe an essentially theological problem. Does man dare to judge Deity?" And of course he must, if he is to remain a man.

20. B. Vawter, *Job and Jonah*, 8, "There is no God, in any meaningful sense of the word, unless he is understood by men".

21. A point made by Karl Jaspers. See J. Collins, *The Existentialists. A Critical Study*, Chicago, 1952, 249.

22. According to Kierkegaard, who sees in the "young Elihu" the *idealism* of faith. Having no experience, the young can afford the luxury of being idealists. The older man, who has experienced life, sees that there are cracks in the picture of God. *Diary*, II, 230.

23. J.S. Dunne, *A Search for God in Time and Memory*, London, 1975, 40. One finds something very similar in Beckett's *Waiting for Godot*. Vladimir, when he questions the second boy, realizes that the Godot he has constructed has been built on the same lines as the traditional "God" of Judaeo-Christianity – figure representing absolute power and ultimate meaning – and that this figure is as futile as the traditional one. See also E. Webb, *The Plays of Samuel Beckett*, 40.

24. A point made by Karl Barth, "Der wahrhaftige Zeuge", in *Die Kirchliche Dogmatik*, Zürich, 1949–1970, IV, 443–499. Barth dedicates a major section of vol. IV of his major work to the *Book of Job* under the general rubric of the falsehood of man.

25. H. Knight, "Job, considered as a contribution to Hebrew theology", in *SJTh*9(1956), 73. This is important to all theology which, in Israel as elsewhere, has a tendency to project a familiar, and so comforting, image of the Creator: one who governs his world according to *ma'at*; a vindicator, a righteous judge. In the end, a God one can come to terms with.

26. In his *Pensées*, Pascal notes: "Dieu étant ainsi caché, toute religion qui ne

dit pas que Dieu est caché n'est pas véritable; et toute religion qui n'en rend pas la raison n'est pas instruisante. La nôtre fait tout cela: *Vere tu es Deus Absconditus.*" Paris, 1946, 291.

27. "In the very excess of his suffering lies man's claim to dignity. Powerless and broken, a blind beggar hounded out of the city [Cadmus] assumes a new grandeur. Man is ennobled by the vengeful spite or injustice of the gods." G. Steiner, *The Death of Tragedy*, 9–10.

PART III

THE THEOPHANY: 38:1–42:6
THE SECOND POLE OF THE PROVERB:
HOW GOD SEES HIMSELF

Chapter 6

God's vision of absurdity

Given the structure of the debate (3–31), God has no choice: he must respond. The reader expects it of him. The convincing force of Job's argument, no less than the emphasis on his request for legal confrontation in the last three chapters of the Dialogue, forces Yahweh's hand. Likewise, the fact that the first pole of the *mashal* ends, formally, with an oath of clearance forces the issue: if God does not respond, he is tacitly admitting he is at fault. So answer he must, and his appearance in theophany opens the second part of the proverb – God as he sees himself.

Indeed, this is inevitable both structurally and dramatically. The "proverb" form demands at least two poles of comparison, two options for the reader. If Job has presented reason's portrait of divinity, what is the alternative? There has to be one if the book is to be more than an existential cry in the dark. It is natural for the average human being to identify with Job's complaint, and so without a contrast and a counter-argument the reader would be left with nothing to stretch his mind, to *provoke* him into re-assessing the familiar human argument of a cruel God in the light of an alternative vision, and so the theological process would be aborted. Furthermore, the authenticity of the Yahweh Speeches is borne out by the unity of language; the high poetic level of the Dialogue is, for the most part, maintained into the Theophany, and indeed key poetic and dramatic elements of the Dialogue are found again in the speeches of God, seemingly from the same hand.[1] So the literary integrity of the book demands some answer. Job is so utterly convinced that innocence *can* challenge God and *can* indict him[2] that a reader begins to wonder – "has God not perhaps got a point of view of his own, even a good and valid answer?" The fact is that he has been psychologically set up. So has God. He has no choice but to respond and present his own side of the case.

He does so, in chapters 38–42, and a very strange argument it is:

> Then the Lord answered Job out of the whirlwind:
> "Who is this that darkens counsel by words without knowl-
> edge?
> Gird up your loins like a man,
> I will question you, and you shall declare to me."
>
> (38:1–3)

So strange is the content of the double speech that follows that it has been suggested it amounts to a form of brutal irony or verbal bullying on God's part.[3] If so, it is more heavy-handed than one should expect from the author of the poetry of 3–31: "Have you got an arm like God? Have you given orders to the morning? Can you fasten the harness of the Pleiades, or untie Orion's bands?" It is less than justice to the author to take seriously the idea that the poetry of chapters 38–41 represents either verbal irony or sarcasm on the part of God – it is too powerfully constructed for that, and such a literary tactic would not have been convincing to a contemporary reader. Nor is it simply a gracious condescension on God's part; the firmly logical sequence and the tightly-knit structural pattern responds too closely to the tenor of the Dialogue.[4] Two carefully woven speeches of Yahweh stand in dialectical polarity with the equally carefully structured Jobian argument of the Dialogue.

The sequence of questions addressed by God to Job serves a precise educational purpose. The God of the Theophany is using a form of Socratic interrogative style to make the reader look again at the protagonist's argument, and see it from a different point of view. In the complex of the whole *Book of Job* the Theophany represents more than simply an experience Job himself had of his Creator;

it is an argument addressed to a reader. Man can criticize God: that is the ultimate privilege of his autonomy. He can judge what he sees God do. But that judgement must be assessed and controlled by viewing it from a different perspective. Every thesis must be in tension with an antithesis. So, after the rational journey through the world of traditional theology the author now leads us on an imaginative journey through the world of natural wonders – a journey through the Land of Oz.

A journey through the land of the absurd

The two speeches that make up the Theophany re-introduce the reader to the world of fable found in the Prologue. The symbolism is heavily mythological: the founding of the earth on pillars (38:4–7), and taming of the sea (38:8–11) and the moulding of earth (38:12–15), the search for the gates of death and the dwelling of light and darkness (38:16–21). We are dealing with the primeval, mythological origins of things. Day suggests that 38:8–11 is based on a creation psalm (104), and retails God's battle to gain control over the personified sea at the time of creation. Stylistically it is very similar to Canaanite mythology of creation where the primordial powers of Chaos, Yam and Tannin, are controlled by Marduk.[5]

The two speeches are marked out by two explicit points of interrogation, two divine questions that highlight the content of the speeches: knowledge (38:2) and control (40:9):

> Who is this who darkens my design
> with words without knowledge? . . . . . .

> Do you have power like God,
> can you thunder with a voice like his?

Within this interlocutory one finds three blocks of poetry:[6]

38:2–38:   cosmology (mythological)

97

38:39–39:30: the irrational world of creation (reality)
40:15–41:34: the uncontrollable power of Behemoth and
Leviathan (mythological)

The worlds of myth and of reality are brilliantly inter-
woven. By a simple stroke of the divine artist's brush Job
stands revealed as one who is incapable of fathoming the
mysteries of nature and of coping with the seeming chaos
of creation. But he is also one who is capable of *contemplat-
ing* this fact.

A *vision of unreason*

The nature of God's response has shifted Job's attention, and that of the reader, from man to God, from inexplicable suffering and the nature of the human condition
to God and his view of the world.

> Who is this who darkens my design
>   with words without knowledge? . . .
> Where were you when I laid the foundation of the earth?
>   Tell me, if you have understanding.
> Who determined its measurements – surely you know!
>   Or who stretched the line upon it?
> On what were its bases sunk,
>   or who laid its cornerstone,
> when the morning stars sang together,
>   and all the sons of God shouted for joy?
> Or who shut in the sea with doors,
>   when it burst forth from the womb;
> when I made clouds its garment,
>   and thick darkness its swaddling band,
> and prescribed bounds for it,
>   and set bars and doors,
> and said, "Thus far shall you come, and no farther,
>   and here shall your proud waves be stayed"?
>
> (38:2, 4–11)

Earlier on, in *his* opening gambit, Job had sought to
reverse creation; now Yahweh, in terms equally dramatic,
re-asserts it.[7] There are several interesting elements in this
introduction to the fabulous world of creation. In both

38:4 and 39:26 Job's lack of *knowledge* is underlined, his inability to understand the world around him and to find any rational pattern to it. But there is more than a hint here of the moral dimension of life as well. This appears under the skin of the text in 38:12–15:

> Have you commanded the morning since your days began,
>   and caused the dawn to know its place,
> that it might take hold of the skirts of the earth,
>   and the wicked be shaken out of it?
> It is changed like clay under the seal,
>   and it is dyed like a garment.
> From the wicked their light is withheld,
>   and their uplifted arm is broken.

To the Hebrew, and clearly to the author of the *Book of Job*, day and night are not simply temporal poles, but represent also a moral polarity. By his ability to bring light into being and thereby drive back darkness it seems that Yahweh is also implying that he, and only he, can and does control evil: "have you commanded the morning to arrive, and thereby uprooted the wicked from the place they have usurped?" Yahweh can and does deal with moral inequity – at his own time and in his own way. The light of dawn represents God's exclusive power to regulate human life and activity,[8] and here Job's control cannot reach. The protagonist is reminded that he who had called down the curse of annihilation on day and night in *his* opening speech (chapter 3) cannot even *find* either of them. Job had claimed that death and Sheol would be preferable to life, but he had never visited that dismal place and so could not have made such a choice intelligently. As C.S. Lewis observes (in his *Narnia* tales), only the ignorant would search for the "Island where Dreams come True". What if they found it? If one realized what death and Sheol implied one would never choose that land. To do so, one must have an overwhelming reason for the choice.

The second block of creation poetry begins at 38:39[9] and introduces the familiar world of nature. But even that world – how "familiar" is it after all? Once again, Yahweh has shifted the perspective on a world once thought familiar and shown that hand-in-hand with its breath-taking splendour goes its irrationality. The hunting lion, the bird of prey, the free-moving mountain goat and wild ass are spectacular, but they all live in a blood-soaked world where predators stalk their innocent victims, and kill to live. The inanimate cosmos was treated in the language of myth (chapter 38), now the world of nature is treated realistically, as Yahweh presents the world he created, and more than hints at its relationship to himself (creator) and to man (fellow creature):

> Can you hunt the prey for the lion,
>   or satisfy the appetite of the young lions,
> when they crouch in their dens,
>   or lie in wait in their covert?
> Who provides for the raven its prey,
>   when its young ones cry to God,
>   and wander about for lack of food?
>
> Do you know when the mountain
>   goats bring forth?
> Do you observe the calving of the hinds?
> Can you number the months that they fulfil,
>   and do you know the time when they bring forth,
> when they crouch, bring forth their offspring,
>   and are delivered of their young?
> Their young ones become strong, they grow up in the open;
>   they go forth, and do not return to them.
>
> Who has let the wild ass go free?
>   Who has loosed the bonds of the swift ass,
> to whom I have given the steppe for his home,
>   and the salt land for his dwelling place?
> He scorns the tumult of the city;
>   he hears not the shouts of the driver.
> He ranges the mountains as his pasture,
>   and he searches after every green thing.
>
> Is the wild ox willing to serve you?
>   Will he spend the night at your crib?
> Can you bind him in the furrow with ropes,
>   or will he harrow the valleys after you?
> Will you depend on him because his strength is great,
>   and will you leave to him your labour?

Do you have faith in him that he will return,
and bring your grain to your threshing floor?

(38:39–39:12)

Beauty and cruelty belong together. Indeed, they are necessary complements to each other:

Is it by your wisdom that the hawk soars,
and spreads his wings toward the south?
Is it at your command that the eagle mounts up
and makes his nest on high?
On the rock he dwells and makes his home
in the fastness of the rocky crag.
Thence he spies out the prey;
his eyes behold it afar off.
His young ones suck up blood;
and where the slain are, there is he.

(39:26–30)

God has so arranged it that splendour and suffering are inseparable. One creature kills another to live; one dies so that another may be born. And the human species is part of this balance. Indeed, he himself is the ultimate predator – who is there to prey on him, and preserve the delicate balance? God?

What is certainly communicated by this poetry is man's essential limitation – he has a short span of days; he has not created the environment in which he lives; his knowledge is inadequate to control it or make sense of it. Indeed, Yahweh was right: "Can you bind the chains of the Pleiades, or loose the bonds of Orion? Can you bring forth the constellations in their due time or guide the Bear with its young?"

The search for such an astrological taxonomy is, in the ancient Near East, a search for ultimate knowledge; a search for wisdom and control – a thirst that is never slaked.

Yahweh's second speech opens with another challenge, but the wording is significantly different to the first challenge of 38:2.

Would you even try to put me in the wrong,
and condemn me, that you may justify yourself?

Indeed, do you think you have an arm like God,
and can even thunder with a voice like his?

(40:8–9)

The argument has moved from cosmic design to control:
"will you even *discredit my mishpat* . . .?" In the Hebrew
text of v. 8 the term *mishpat* is used, and this signifies
governance and control. Here in the Theophany it is used
cosmically. God's *mishpat*, his "judgement" or "control",
is not confined to the administration of justice, to reward or
retribution, as Job had consistently seen it in the Dialogue.
Rather it is his responsibility and capacity for cosmic
governance and control.[10] Once again in the divine answer
to Job a "familiar" concept is presented in a different light,
from a different point of view – this time, God's. It is no
longer a question of forensic justice in his treatment of the
human creature, as it had been when Job accused God of
injustice – that is, of acting contrary to right reason.
Yahweh knows there is "innocent" suffering, injustice and
inequity in the world, but it may be deemed "reasonable"
(if the word means anything) when viewed from where he
stands. That is, it may take on a positive value. To prove
this argument, the reader is once more led into the world
of myth and introduced to two fabulous beasts:

Behold, Behemoth,
　　which I made as I made you;
　　he eats grass like an ox.
Behold, his strength in his loins,
　　and his power in the muscles of his belly.
He makes his tail stiff like a cedar;
　　the sinews of his thighs are knit together.
His bones are tubes of bronze,
　　his limbs like bars of iron.

He is the first of the works of God;
　　let him who made him bring near his sword!
For the mountains yield food for him
　　where all the wild beasts play.
Under the lotus plants he lies,
　　in the covert of the reeds and in the marsh.
For his shade the lotus trees cover him;
　　the willows of the brook surround him.

102

Behold, if the river is turbulent he is not frightened;
    he is confident though Jordan rushes against his mouth.
Can one take him with hooks,
    or pierce his nose with a snare?

Can you draw out Leviathan with a fishhook,
    or press down his tongue with a cord?
Can you put a rope in his nose,
    or pierce his jaw with a hook?
Will he make many supplications to you?
    Will he speak to you soft words?
Will he make a covenant with you
    to take him for your servant for ever?
Will you play with him as with a bird,
    or will you put him on leash for your maidens?
Will traders bargain over him?
    Will they divide him up among the merchants?
Can you fill his skin with harpoons,
    or his head with fishing spears?
Lay hands on him;
    think of the battle; you will not do it again!
Behold, the hope of a man is disappointed;
    he is laid low even at the sight of him.
No one is so fierce that he dares to stir him up.
    Who then is he that can stand before me?

                              (40:15–41:10)

There is disagreement among authors as to the identity of these two creatures, some seeing them as natural animals belonging to the taxonomy that began with the lion in 38:39; but given the linguistic and stylistic context it seems more likely that they represent the mythical forces of Near Eastern literature.[11] Certainly Leviathan, in one linguistic form or another, is understood as a representative of primeval Chaos that God had to overcome in his act of creation. This is especially evident in the Psalms.[12] Behemoth and Leviathan together form, as it were, a single picture. The depiction of Behemoth, as it is found here in 40:15–24 is almost a still-life, a formalized picture like an Egyptian wall-painting, and Leviathan is described in similar terms, though not in as much detail as is Behemoth.[13] The two form a unit, having only one introduction, and so the two pictures present one complex image of uncontrollable power, derived from the subconscious mythology of the race.[14] They are introduced in 40:15 with the poetic flourish of the storyteller:

> See now! Behemoth,
> whom I formed as I formed you.

It is a poetic convention, calling a reader's attention to a symbolic utterance. By thus linking Job with Behemoth the reader is expected to compare the two – man and mythic beast – throughout the whole poem. The same is true of Leviathan. He is a paradigm of man's powerlessness in the face of a created universe of which he constitutes no more than a part. In the earlier text of chapter 3:8 Leviathan is clearly more than a natural animal; he represents the powers of Chaos that threaten creation and that stand beyond man's control.[15] But he is not beyond God's control. Like all the rest, from lion to eagle (38:39; 39:27), he stands within the context of God's lordship over all of creation. Both Behemoth and Leviathan are representative of the Chaos from which Yahweh draws order and meaning.[16] Thus the major statement made about Behemoth is crucial to the author's intention:

> He is the first of all the works of God.

> (40:19a)

The terminology (*re'shit darkê-'el* in Hebrew) inevitably draws the reader's mind to Prov 8:22 where Wisdom was first of all God's works. Thus, since Behemoth symbolizes the powers of Chaos, the fact that he is the "first created" would suggest that, as Yahweh sees things, the world was created chaotic. Chaos is its basic nature. The moral law and the natural law are in disharmony.[17] And it is Yahweh who underlines this fact. Why look for reason? There is none. There is only a strange beauty beyond reason.

Acknowledging the "plan" of God

With dramatic integrity, the author presents his protagonist's final response in such a way as to confirm this:

Who is this who obscures counsel without knowledge?
Indeed I have spoken about things I did not understand,
marvels beyond me and beyond my knowledge.

(42:3)

This text is a masterpiece of ambiguity. Two words are carefully balanced in the Hebrew text of v. 3: "obscures", or better "hides" (*ma'lîm*) and "without *knowledge*" (*da'at*). The word for "hides" comes from the root *'lm*, which means "that which is hidden". In the light of the divine argument Job acknowledges that indeed he is one who has caused God's "plan" to be "hidden" or "obscured" because, without "knowledge", that is experiential knowledge, the plan or design had been hidden from him. He had not known that "reason" existed at the heart of divine unreason.

The author is deliberately playing on words. Yahweh's challenge in 38:2 had spoken of Job "darkening" (*mah-shîk*) knowledge; Job instead confesses to having been blind to it (*ma'lîm*). His argument in 3:31 had "darkened" God's project, because he had not known, from experience, that all of this unreasonable state of suffering, all the absurdity of human alienation, *did* really add up to a divine project. He had not suspected the existence of a design that could incorporate absurdity. Thus what the protagonist concedes, at the end of the divine argument, is that God's "projects" (*mezimmâ*, 42:2), always work out. So unreason is part of a divine purpose, a projected goal; and it is this that is in question in the second speech from the storm, and not simply divine governance or divine control. "Are you able to govern better than me?" is *not* God's question, as might be thought from a reading of 40:9 ("has your arm the strength of God's, can your voice thunder as loud?"). But rather, "I have a project that you do not *know of*": *yada'*, the verb used in 42:2 is frequently used by both Job and Yahweh.[18] What is in question is not God's (or Job's) *power* to bring about projects but the fact of God *having* projects that are not perceptible to human reason. After the two divine speeches Job has seen so many mysteries, so many "irrational" and "meaningless" won-

105

ders, actually weave a poetic tapestry in God's hands, that he can acknowledge he has been looking at it all from the wrong point of view. So Job succumbs, as both friends and readers guessed he would, and Yahweh reveals his ignorance as the reader had expected and even Job may have subconsciously feared. The "submission", however, is not to authority or power, but to mystery.[19]

Job had claimed to see nothing but absurdity in the created world; God agrees, drawing a picture of the mythic and the irrational in the world of experience. Yet even in that vision of absurdity there are real values and a creative balance. Even the Absurd has its function. Neither rain nor dew are organized or directed (38:25-27). They serve no purpose except to bring a fleeting beauty to a desert where no one lives. What happens in nature "makes no sense", but God has his own reasons for the destructive elements that threaten the human environment – perhaps simply to create something beautiful, like a flowering desert. Perhaps he has no other purpose than creating something *good in itself*, and not simply *good for* man. The lion and the raven (38:39f) are awe-inspiring and majestic – but both are professional killers. In the order of nature Yahweh has to concur in the spilling of "innocent" blood: one creature lives off the flesh of another – yet this fact does not detract from the majesty of the lion: indeed, it may enhance it – a creature beautiful *and dangerous*, all the more beautiful, perhaps, *because* dangerous. Of what value to man is the hawk, conjured up by the poetry of 39:26-30? Purely aesthetic, as "useless" as the poem that brings him to life for others:

> Is it by your wisdom that the hawk soars,
>   and spreads his wings towards the south?
> Is it at your command that the eagle mounts up
>   and makes his nest on high?

The ostrich is a "foolish bird", apt to destroy her own offspring inadvertently – yet what more majestic in motion as she outstrips the horse (39:13f)? The horse, like the lion, is glorious in his power (39:19f), stronger than man yet willing to serve him; and the hawk in flight passes human understanding, effortlessly doing the impossible. The eagle is another contradiction, an innocent killer. God has deliberately worked contradiction and absurdity into the fabric of his creation, which is maintained and perfected by the very dialectic of contradiction.

All of this is true of the moral sphere also:

> Will you even put me in the wrong?
> > Will you condemn me that you may be justified?
> Have you an arm like God,
> > and can you thunder with a voice like his?
>
> Deck yourself with majesty and dignity;
> > clothe yourself with glory and splendour.
> Pour forth the overflowings of your anger,
> > and look on every one that is proud, and abase him.
> Look on every one that is proud, and bring him low;
> > and tread down the wicked where they stand.
> Hide them all in the dust together;
> > bind their faces in the world below.
> Then will I also acknowledge to you,
> > that your own right hand can give you victory.
>
> (40:8–14)

Yahweh, in a way, is conceding that he cannot just summarily dispose of the wicked and the unrighteous – for even they are part of the cosmic whole. They represent, perhaps, the liberty that God has inserted into creation – freedom implies the capacity to do wrong. In fact, Karl Barth suggests that this says quite a lot about the nature of the divinity:[20] the "unjust" God of experience is also the God of faith; the God who creates beauty and joy is also the God who imposes suffering and pain as man's natural lot. Can beauty exist without tension, poetry without pain? It is to this "vision of unreason" that Job responds:

> Then Job answered Yahweh, saying:
> "I know you can do all things and no project of yours can be thwarted.
> > [you asked] 'who is this who obscures counsel without knowledge?'
> > Indeed, I have spoken about things I did not understand, marvels beyond me and beyond my knowledge.
> 'Listen now, and I will speak [you said];

I will question you and you must answer me.'
By the hearing of the ear I had heard of you,
  but now my eyes have seen you.
Therefore I despise myself [I retract]
  and repent in [on account of] dust and ashes."

(42:1–6)

But what does the response mean? It stands as one of the most ambiguous texts in the whole book, and as such presents major problems of interpretation. Is the protagonist submitting to God's argument, or is he entrenching himself more stubbornly in his attitude of rebellion?[21] What appears from a first reading is the fact that twice he quotes Yahweh's challenge, and each time adds a personal rider:

3a = "who is this who obscures counsel without knowledge?" is a reprise of 38:2.

3b = "I spoke about things I did not *understand, marvels beyond me* and beyond my *knowledge*".

4 = "I will question you and you must answer me" is a reprise of both 38:3 and 40:7.

5 = "By the hearing of the ear I had heard of you, but now my eyes have seen you".

It is as a result of *this* argument that v. 6 presents his "submission":

6 = Therefore I despise myself [?]
    and repent in dust and ashes [?].

It is clear that in each case Job's perception of what constituted his "error", or his argument in the light of the Theophany, is crucial to the reader's interpretation of the whole "proverb" of Job – the human argument and the divine.

Verse 3b consists of two half-lines that communicate the first part of Job's reaction to the divine challenge. The Hebrew text is a masterpiece of equivocation, and can be rendered in several ways:

1. Job has submitted unconditionally, repenting of his former attitude..

108

2. Job is pretending to submit, because it is not worth arguing with a God who can do nothing but blister.
3. Job, angered by God's dishonesty in debate and his contempt for fallible humankind resolves to continue in his opposition, and regrets even the semblance of submission.

One modern exegete, Patrick, sees "beyond my knowledge" and "things I did not understand" (v. 3) simply as interjections expressing amazement, while another, Morrow, discussing this agrees that "to *speak* about things", or "to utter" (from the verbal root *ngd*) often appears in a context of an exclamation of praise or wonder.[22] Perhaps Job has recognized by now that his earlier attitude of confrontation was wrong since God's speech has brought the essential mystery and irrationality of creation to his attention. So he is set to abandon his previous position. But for what? One would expect v. 6 to solve the problem, but in fact while the text is clear enough the meaning is not. In Hebrew the grammatical form of the words here translated as "I despise myself", and "I repent in dust and ashes" allows for several interpretations. "I despise" has in fact no object, and can scarcely be used reflexively, while "repent in" (used reflexively) can mean "repent of" my previous attitude of docility – "dust and ashes". Scarcely a submission; more like an attitude of disgust. Repenting "in dust and ashes" is also open to several interpretations, since the word used quite often means "change one's mind", and the Targum renders v. 6 as "therefore I am totally reduced, since I am no more than dust and ashes", that is, a frail, limited human being.[23] If the divine speeches are interpreted as an *argumentum ad hominem* (as they are by some authors), then v. 6 could easily be interpreted as Job's repudiation of God's dishonesty in argument: "If that is your way of doing things, then I, Job, am sorry for frail man whom you created so circumscribed and on whom you impose your prepotence".

There are almost as many interpretations of this last "submission" as there are exegetes – and this may well be the deliberate intention of the author. For this is a carefully written piece of poetry, and it shows all the signs of a writer who knew what he was doing. It would appear, from this text and from several others in the book, that the author liked to present statements that could be interpreted in a variety of ways, dependent on how a particular reader understood a particular text. Very like a *mashal*, in fact. So it is possible that the author has worked a deliberate ambiguity into this final "submission" or final statement. In the light of God's argument, is Job retracting his previously held opinion, is he simply holding his tongue, or is he even walking away in disgust from an adversary who will not come to terms with an honestly expressed opinion? The answer depends on the reader. There is no apodictic solution offered by the *Book of Job* – it is a *mashal*, a proverb offering two points of view to a reader who, knowing the situation of innocent suffering, can contemplate two arguments – the human and the divine. Depending on his assessment, and of course his natural sympathies, he decides.

Like every literary classic from the Agammemnon to Hamlet, the *Book of Job* is a challenge to the reader who, in the light of his own experience, becomes his own interpreter.

NOTES

1. See Terrien, *Job*, 27f; Dhorme, *A Commentary on the Book of Job*, lxxxv; Habel, *The Book of Job*, 32f. Robert Alter notes that the Yahweh Speeches are, *in the force of their poetry*, "so intricately and so powerfully a fulfillment of key elements in the body of the poetic argument": *The Art of Biblical Poetry*, New York, 1985, 88.
2. See J.L. Crenshaw, *A Whirlpool of Torment*, 62.
3. Pope, *Job*, xxvii, comments that some authors "see in it only brutal irony and utter lack of concern for man's predicament". See also H.H. Rowley, *Job*, 242f.
4. See Alter, *The Art of Biblical Poetry*, 86. Many authors feel that the very fact of God responding to Job in his suffering is sufficient a grace for him: see Rowley, *Job*, 20; F.I. Andersen, *Job. An Introduction and Commentary*, Leicester, 1976, 269; A. Weiser, *Das Buch Hiob*, 22f.
5. J. Day, *God's Conflict with the dragon and the sea. Echoes of a Canaanite myth in the Old Testament*, Cambridge, 1985, 43. The creation myth in question is found in *Enuma Ekish*, IV,110f.
6. L. Alonso Schökel & J.L. Sicre Diaz, *Job*, 608f. See also P.W. Skehan,

Studies in Israelite Poetry and Wisdom (CBQMS), Washington, 1971, 120, who suggests a variant of this.

7. R. Alter, *Art of Biblical Poetry*, 96, sees this as a deliberate reference back to Job's speech in chapter 3.

8. In this regard see Habel, *op. cit.*, 548.

9. M.V. Fox, "Job 38 and God's Rhetoric", in *Semeia* 19(1981), 56.

10. Habel, *The Book of Job*, 562. See also W. Whedbee, "The Comedy of Job", in *Semeia* 7(1977), 25.

11. Pope, *Job*, xxvii.

12. According to J. Day, *God's Conflict with the dragon and the sea*, 18f, the idea of Leviathan associated with the Chaoskampf is found in Ps 74; 89; 104; 65; 93, and perhaps 24 and 29.

13. See H. Richter, "Die Naturweisheit des Alten Testaments im Buche Hiob", in *ZAW* 70(1958), 3 and J.E. Hartley, *The Book of Job*, Grand Rapids, 1988, 521.

14. See for example Enoch 60:7–8; 4 Ezra 6:49–52; Apoc. of Baruch 11:29. W. Lillie, "The Religious Significance of the Theophany in the Book of Job", in *ExpT* 68(1957), 356.

15 R. Alter, *The Art of Biblical Poetry*, 12, makes an interesting statement in this line though with reference to another text. The principle applies here equally. See also Habel, *The Book of Job*, 558, and H. Rowland, "Leviathan and Job in Job 41:2–3", in *JBL* 105(1986), 106.

16. The parallels from Ugaritic literature support this view. See Ps 74 and Is 27.

17. D. Robertson, *The Old Testament and the Literary Critic*, Philadelphia, 1977, 50f.

18. See the point made in Alonso Schökel & Diaz, *Job*, 671f. For the nuances of meaning suggested by the difficult grammar of this section, see also W. Baumgartner & J.J. Stamm, *Hebräisches und Aramäisches Lexikon zum Alten Testament*, 789f: the form of the verb is hifil participle.

19. Given the trial atmosphere of the confession of 42:2. See also Ravasi, *Giobbe*, who cites Richter in this regard. See also Robertson, *The Old Testament and the Literary Critic*, 52f. T.S. Eliot's *Murder in the Cathedral*, while not itself a work of mythology, presents a protagonist who likewise submits to mystery rather than to authority: see R.Y. Hathorn, *Tragedy, Myth and Mystery*, 36f.

20. A. Brenner, "God's Answer to Job", in *VT* 31(1981), 133. Also Habel, *The Book of Job*, 542f. Again, Barth presents one of the problems of the book quite intuitively in volume IV of his *Kirchliche Dogmatik*.

21. To judge the arguments for and against this conclusion it will be worth looking at R. Gordis, *The Book of Job*, 573; Alonso Schökel and Diaz, *Job*, 60; D. Patrick, "The Translation of Job XLII 6" in *VT* 26(1976), 371, and J.B. Curtis, "On Job's Response to Yahweh", in *JBL* 98(1979), 501.

22. D. Patrick, "The Translation of Job CLII 6", 371; W. Morrow, "Consolation, Rejection, and Repentance in Job 42,6", in *JBL* 105(1986), 222, and Gordis, *Book of Job*, 573.

23. Patrick, *op. cit.*, 369, Curtis, *loc. cit.*, and Morrow, *op. cit.*, 212.

Chapter 7

What has the theophany achieved?

The two speeches by Yahweh leave the reader hanging in the air. Most contemporary scholars agree that this Theophany hardly represents a *response* to Job's argument, since in fact it is not primarily concerned to *refute* what was said in the Dialogue.

It is really a *parallel argument*. Looking at the same phenomenon of the human condition and its existential absurdity, God simply sees it from a different angle. He is saying, in effect: "Very well, you think your perception of reality is the right one? Now listen to my point of view." Quite often agreeing with Job's perception of the world, Yahweh sees it as mystery rather than absurdity. Thus the second part of the *mashal* of Job ends in tension – but a different tension to that in which the Dialogue ends.[1] If Job now agrees with this divine argument he has to deny the validity of his own argument from experience, and in a way so does the reader. For one thing is obvious: there is no human being, having a mature experience of life and its moral complexity, its inequality, its injustice, its meaningless pain, who does not feel sympathy for the Jobian vision presented in chapters 3–31. For this reason, it is really the Dialogue that carries the drama; the Theophany simply adds a new point of view. But it is upon the reader's acceptance or not of this point of view, and naturally on his understanding of its meaning, that the significance of the book as a whole depends. The "God" of Job and the "God" of the friends have been represented: now the Theophany has given Yahweh's "God". It may not be necessary to accept this concept of the divinity, but it is essential to see it as an antithesis to the Jobian (and human) thesis of 3–31 – a "negative", perhaps, to set off the "positive" of the Dialogue.

Polarity is essential to drama and to the functioning of thought. Without a dialectic of thesis-antithesis such as is provided by the "proverb" form there is no urgency to re-think an accepted concept, either of God or man. Thus in a way chapters 3–31 is the *real* book, the "book of man's experience", and 38–41 is a pole of comparison, a foil to give the reader a point of reference for his own independent thinking; a challenge to existential theology, as it were, for there will be no conflict in his mind if he is given only an argument he identifies with. So without 38–41 he would not be challenged to think of the possibility of there being an alternative point of view.

Thus it is crucial to see the book as a whole, and structured as it now is, just as the final author or editor presents it: Prologue, Dialogue, Theophany, Epilogue. It is clearly destined for a reader,[2] and so the final author saw a coherence in it as he left it, and indeed intended it to be read as it stands. What is most important here is the fact that it ends *without an answer* – to the problem of innocent suffering or to the absurdity of the human condition – so responding to these questions is not the primary scope of the work. What it does is present God as he is perceived by man and as he perceives himself. The only "answer" is the one the reader finds for himself as he contemplates the *mashal* of the *Book of Job* and asks the question: "what kind of God . . ." How does the Theophany contribute to the answer?

The Socratic style of the divine argument

There is a great deal of debate about what God is doing in these two speeches, and what their literary genre is. The language used by Yahweh would at first suggest that he is being heavily ironic, if not downright sarcastic, particularly in the first speech (38–39).

114

Where were you when I laid earth's foundations?
Have you ever commanded the morning?
Have you traced the storehouse of the snow?
Can you bind the Pleiades,
    or loose the bonds of Orion?

If heavy irony were the author's intention it would destroy the dramatic integrity of the divine speeches. What function would it serve to portray God as a comedian playing to the gallery? Even the desire to beat Job to his knees in submission would contribute more to farce than to tragedy.[3] In fact, Job's submission can scarcely be due to his being overwhelmed by God's power and control and so being found to realize that his anthropocentric argument was inadequate and his judgement on the divinity presumptuous. Neither Job nor the reader could be so foolish.

There is something else to the Theophany besides this – an alternative to the conceptual tradition that limited God's role to that of creator, wise governor and just judge. Even in his revolt Job had repeatedly returned, as with nostalgia, to this ideal; now God's view of himself shatters the image. For this reason there has to be an *objective* meaning to the divine speeches, a conceptual content *to what Yahweh says*. It is not sufficient to say that the "experience" of God in itself had value for the protagonist. The meaning of what God says must be both perceptible to a reader and related to the Jobian argument contained in the Dialogue. Job had wished to meet God on man's terms – he had sought vindication in a "trial of innocence" against an unjust judge, for it was as a creator judge he saw the divinity. For this reason his forensic "either-or" argument – "If I am innocent you must be guilty" – made sense. But it had been too judicial by far,[4] and too tied to a monolithic concept of God. Because of this the "lawsuit" theme that dominates the latter half of the Dialogue was doomed to failure. Were God to meet man thus, on man's terms alone, in a courtroom dominated by human reason, he would have to abdicate his own nature for he would be accepting man's limited conception of him. Job would have God act, as he himself does, with justice; Yahweh acts with

115

more than justice – he acts with creative imagination. So in *his* speeches Yahweh transfers the argument from its judicial framework to its creational. In a way, the divine argument does represent a response to Job's lawsuit as 40:2 suggests with its double use of forensic terminology[5]:

Will he who *contends* with God even correct him,
will God's *accuser* be able to answer him?

but the ground of the debate has subtly altered. Job's argument had been that God's treatment of his creation was chaotic and unjust; God's answer is, "Of course! I am not a judge, I am an artist". Therefore, *in its way*, when looked at from a different angle, God's activity is both controlled and moral, and more, it is fabulous.

Many authors contend that Yahweh is forcing Job to submit, simply on the basis of the fact that the divine speeches are stylistically dominated by the question form: "where were you when I laid the foundations of the earth?", "have you entered the springs of the sea?" – all unanswerable. Particularly in the first speech (38–39) the main rhetorical technique is this piling up of questions, and this is neither ornamental nor polemical. It is a deliberate teaching device. By this rhetoric of interrogation, the use of questions that are also statements in question form, a dynamic of communication is set up: each of them, interrogator and interrogated, knows what the only answer can be, and is aware of the other's knowledge. A relationship of shared cognition is established. Yahweh is drawing Job into the dialectic of thesis-antithesis, making him see the same familiar world in different colours. Ricoeur points out that in the beginning of each movement there is concrete imagery controlled by a question,[6] the whole implication being: "Do you *know* or *understand* what I am showing you?", the answer being: "Of course you do not *know* or *understand*." It is remarkable that verbs for "knowing" or "understanding" occur ten times in the first, cosmological, part of the first speech, chapter 38: *Do you know* how I laid the foundations of the earth? *Do you know* the expanse of the earth? *Do you know* the way to the dwelling of light? *Do you know* the ordering of the heavens? All of these are mysteries, yet man never questions them. Why, then, does he question suffering and injustice, equally mysteries?

The divine speeches are thus neither verbal irony nor bullying. They are educational shock-tactics, as were the Socratic Dialogues. It is here that the key to the *mashal* lies. The proverb form does not really set out to teach in any direct sense. It is not apodictic. The reader or hearer is meant to infer a truth and build an ethic by inference from the double proposition.[7] God's "justice" had been an ethical category imposed by man, not inferred. Yahweh's answer does not impose an alternative category. It simply places certain aspects of experience and reason before the reader and forces him to draw conclusions of his own. Thus the *mashal* that is the *Book of Job* leaves the reader in the position where he must make his own inference.

Challenging the reader's preconceptions

Seen as a whole, in the form in which it has come down to us, it is possible to suggest that *Job* is conducting an assault on a traditional concept of divinity, in the name of reason. This is in fact a common philosophic and dramatic gambit: Plato has Socrates do it in *Euthyphro*, and Aeschylus does it in the *Agammemnon*. For Job, as for Agammemnon, the ethical choice is between two "evils": for Job, to revolt against a traditional view of the divinity or to abdicate his intellectual conviction based on experience; for the Argive king, to disobey the divinity or to sacrifice his own child. This is a dramatic device that serves both author and audience in the task of distinguishing moral values in a particular context, but the recognition of tragedy in this conflict may serve the reader of a different age by fostering the recognition of a moral dilemma in other areas. The world presented by Aeschylus is an illogical world: one sacrifices a daughter to placate a god, thereby offending another god – and inevitably one pays the price. Yet this world has its own logic: a contingent conflict between two ethical claims *need* not be taken (by a reader) for a logical contradiction. It is often educational. To take an existentialist way out, as does Sartre, by ignoring the perceived contradiction would simply be to diffuse the crisis: no crisis, no personal education to a new maturity, and no enlarged perception of the necessary human condition.[8]

God's argument "from the whirlwind", coming as it does in counterpoint to Job's, presents a more richly human and dramatic element – for the crisis is presented with the clarity of two arguments placed side by side, and it is not diffused by evasion. It should not be in drama, for it cannot be in real life. Indeed, a conflict-free life would be lacking in value and beauty in comparison to a life in which it is possible for conflict to arise, for the very tensions that permit strife are at the same time partly constitutive of the values themselves. One thinks of Sophocles' Antigone in conflict with Creon. Normal theatre with a happy ending – all conflict resolved – allows the reader to go away with his own platitudes unchallenged. Were Job allowed the last word (as with 29–31, for example) it would mean he was right and God wrong. Everyman has triumphed, and the reader agrees with what is after all a picture of the human condition he knows so well from his own experience. So he is not forced to face reality, to question stereotypes, but continues to live comfortably in what is essentially a world of make-believe. He is not challenged, and so is free to cling to his own philosophy, his own point of view, irrespective of whether this corresponds to real life or not. Job, and the reader of the Dialogue who is swept along by the poetry of 3–31, presumes that human life is rational, and so should be explicable. God's speeches make such a situation impossible. It has been suggested[9] that Yahweh's description of animals real and fabulous is in fact a description of God himself. He is not "reasonable" – he is, after all, a poet. And he forces the reader to ask: "What has the book achieved?"

The triumph of integrity over dogma

The Prologue established one incontrovertible fact: Job is a classic "believer in God", "a man who was blameless and upright, who feared God and avoided everything evil" (1:1b). His is therefore a pure, traditional faith.[10] This means that the existential answer to the question posed by the Satan in 1:9 has to be, "Yes, Job *does* revere God for nothing; his *is* a true, gratuitous faith". This is borne out by 1:20–22 and again by the editorial hand at 2:10b:

> Then Job fell upon the ground, and worshipped. And he said, "Naked I came from my mother's womb, and naked shall I return; the Lord gave, and the Lord has taken away; blessed be the name of the Lord." In all this Job did not sin or charge God with wrong.
>
> (1:20b–22)
>
> "Shall we receive good at the hand of God, and shall we not receive evil?" In all this Job did not sin with his lips.
>
> (2:10b)

This being true, the question being raised by the book is not, "what sort of religion has Job?", but rather, "what sort of god is Yahweh?" But from the very beginning of the debate the friends had tried to side-step this line of enquiry in favour of a blind adherence to the familiar, and comfortable, theology they had inherited: the innocent simply do not suffer at the hands of God. This type of argument they could control – it was to be found, classically presented, in every manual of theology and of course every official theologian knew it. But Job was not the product of a priestly school, he was a layman. So he begins with philosophy (chapter 3), and his friends persist in responding with theology (chapters 4–5; 8; 11). Perhaps this explains the rather tangential style of the debate, where the responses are seldom direct answers to previous statements. The interchange of opinions is indirect: it is as if an argument of Eliphaz provokes in Job a personal line of thought which is expressed in words after two or three other interventions. The logic is oriental, not occidental,

119

and this is compounded by the difference between textbook theology and existential "theology".

In chapter 3, the first step in his rational enquiry into the nature of God, Job had ceased to be a part of the world around him. He was the quintessential "Stranger", no longer a part of the ordered religious cosmos that others perceive and inhabit. He now stands outside it, regards it, and judges it to be false. He is at a half-way stage. He has not yet reached the "God-perception" of the same phenomenon of absurdity, but he has taken the first step – that away from the comfort of "received truth". He begins by recognizing that there is something stronger than him, something he cannot master:

> Why is light given to a man whose way is hid,
>   whom God has hedged in?
> For my sighing comes as my bread,
>   and my groanings are poured out like water.
> For the thing that I fear comes upon me,
>   and what I dread befalls me.
> I am not at ease, nor am I quiet;
>   I have no rest; but trouble comes.

(3:23–26)

He neither likes this reality nor controls it, but it is there and he recognizes the fact of its existence. In the face of this, the theology of the friends is reduced to a simple "ethical rationalism":[11] one reaps what one sows, for God is a just judge. In effect, this is the position taken by Eliphaz in his first speech:

> As for me, I would seek God,
>   and to God would I commit my cause;
> who does great things and unsearchable,
>   marvellous things without number:
> he gives rain upon the earth
>   and sends waters upon the fields;
> he sets on high those who are lowly,
>   and those who mourn are lifted to safety.
> He frustrates the devices of the crafty,
>   so that their hands achieve no success.
> He takes the wise in their own craftiness;
>   and the schemes of the wily are brought to a quick end.

120

They meet with darkness in the daytime,
  and grope at noonday as in the night.
But he saves the fatherless from their mouth,
  the needy from the hand of the mighty.
So the poor have hope,
  and injustice shuts her mouth.

(5:8–16)

For the reader, of course, this rationalization is seriously put in doubt by the empiric fact that many innocent people suffer, and many wicked prosper. The basis of traditional faith, that of God as just judge and sovereign, has been compromised. But when one loses God, what is there to fall back on? One's own integrity, simply that; human values of truth and probity. But as Cleanth Brooks observes,[12] in these very human virtues one has already found divinity. "Human integrity" is God's incognito, an alias he sometimes assumes. It manifests a divine reality, though not in religious terms. The Job one meets at the end of the Dialogue is a better person, and a more religious, than the Job of the Prologue. As MacLeish's character observes, caustically though perceptively, "Job on his dung hill, yes. That's human. That makes sense. But this world master, this pious, flatulent, successful man who feasts on turkey and thanks God! – he sickens me!"[13]

Already, by its folk-tale beginning and its dramatic highlighting of the image of a righteous man oppressed by a powerful enemy, the first part of the *mashal* has already achieved two things: Job (Everyman) is clearly the hero, and he claims our intellectual allegiance. *And because of this we expect him to win.* He does not. At least, he does not win the argument, as his submission, twice presented (40:3–5 and 42:2–6) makes clear; but what he *does* win, like blind and exiled Oedipus, is a dignity in defeat more impressive than the prepotence of his conqueror. This must surely be the first impression made on a reader of the tragedy of Job. The hero of the Prologue had lived in a dream-world where everything was balanced and symmetrical; the Job of the Dialogue lives in the real world and, like Everyman whom he represents, looks for a way of dominating it: lament, logic, anger, all are tried, and all

121

that prevails is intellectual integrity. Perhaps Yahweh wins the argument, but even he is forced to acknowledge the greater integrity of his opponent, in what must be one of the strangest "confessions" in biblical literature – the divine repudiation of his own witnesses for the defence:

> After the Lord had spoken these words to Job, the Lord said to Eliphaz the Temanite: "My wrath is kindled against you and against your two friends; for you have not spoken of me what is right, as my servant Job has. Now therefore take seven bulls and seven rams, and go to my servant Job, and offer up for yourselves a burnt offering; and my servant Job shall pray for you, for I will accept his prayer not to deal with you according to your folly; for you have not spoken of me what is right, as my servant Job has."
>
> (42:7–8)

This element of victory through defeat is the heart of drama, for as Steiner points out,[14] the tragic hero, such as Oedipus, Prometheus, or Job, is far more noble a figure than the average, and far closer to the bone of the human condition. But he is at the same time typical. For all his nobility he represents common humanity, since otherwise he would have nothing to say about life or about God. Both Job and the friends had agreed on the absolute sublimity of God, who is above all creation and beyond all understanding, but they react to this premise in different ways: for the friends it means he is always right, and suffering man can therefore not be innocent; for Job, who admits he has, in common with all mankind, sinned on occasion (9:2; 14:4), it is God who cannot be innocent, for the suffering he metes out is excessive. To break the vicious circle of this logic, and to lead the protagonist out of the cage of the absurd, what was necessary was an alternative vision (Yahweh's) that would cast a new light on suffering and alienation.

This is seen in one of Beckett's most powerful plays, *Endgame*, in which two characters are moral prisoners in a closed room outside which seemingly nothing lives. One of them, Clov, catches a glimpse, through the window, of a young boy who represents the possibility that there is life outside. The curtain falls on Clov, "dressed for the road", with his hand on the handle of the door, preparatory to "opening the door of the cell and going", thus making his exit into a possibly alternative world. The Yahweh Speeches serve the same dramatic purpose as Clov's vision of "a little . . . child" seeming alive and real outside the world of the absurd which is all he knew until now.

After the Yahweh Speeches of 38–41, their "alternative world vision" releases both protagonist and reader from the closed circle of the theory of retribution that saw suffering negatively, solely as a punishment for sin. The dialectic of human argument/divine argument resulted in a new theology of suffering. Job's great triumph was to recognize the absurd and challenge the God who caused it; Yahweh's triumph was to make Job "gird his loins and stand up like a man" (38:3 and 40:7), and so move beyond his own point of view to a recognition of the fact that if he had succeeded in fitting suffering into a comprehensible pattern he would have ended up with a human "god" and a much impoverished world. The divine speeches forced him to see with the eyes of the divinity, and to understand the divine purpose in the absurd.

A new "theology" of suffering

Job had wanted to be proved innocent: he was.[15] On the basis of his logic in the Dialogue this would seem to require that God be proved wrong: this does not happen. Thus the divine speeches call in question Job's premise, which is faulty. Innocent suffering does not imply divine injustice. So it implies something else. Almost every character in the drama has been supplying "meanings" for Job's suffering: the friends, Elihu included, "know the reason" for it – even the Satan of the Prologue has an answer. The Yahweh of the Theophany offers none. Instead, his response to Job's anger is meant to demonstrate that the relationship must be placed on a different level – suffering does nothing to close the familiarity between man and God, and does not imply the silence of God. It is simply part of the pattern

– Yahweh's pattern; one that includes man, animals and world of nature. Thus God does not *console* the sufferer, he argues his own case, which is as valid and as "logical" as any the sufferer can propose. Man's anger and God's silence are a form of dialogue.

The human creature is bounded by a world of the senses, of reason; a world where things should "mean something". But who says the world is like that – man? He presumes so at his peril. To ask why the world is as it appears to be is to go around in an existential circle – there is no answer. The real question, as Nemo perceives,[16] has to be "*to what end* is the world as it is? What end does it serve by being so?" To this extent Job has been right in his point of view. His problem had not been suffering as such: he agreed with Eliphaz quite early on that it is man's lot. His problem had been *meaningless* suffering, a divine imposition that was not proportionate, and so had to be meaningless. Eliphaz holds:

> Can mortal man be righteous before God?
>   Can a man be pure before his maker?
> Even in his servants he puts no trust,
>   and his angels he charges with error.
>
> (4:17–18)

> Then Job answered:
> "Truly I know that it is so:
> how can a man be just before God?"
>
> (9:1–2)

Had any meaning been perceptible no restoration such as that of the Epilogue would have been necessary – or rather, the perception of "meaning" in suffering would in itself have been a restoration of his human condition. Thus, to say as Eliphaz does that man is essentially weak and that in comparison to God he is insignificant is no answer:

> Man is born to trouble
>   as the sparks fly upward.
> As for me, I would seek God,
>   and to God would I commit my cause;
> who does great things and unsearchable,
>   marvelous things without number.
>
> (5:7–9)

This is the main thrust of the friends' argument, politely put by Eliphaz but unshakeable. It cannot be God's, though in an interesting way the first friend is foreshadowing one aspect of the divine argument, even if he seems unaware of the implications. Yahweh cannot simply wish to demonstrate man's lack of control or knowledge. Everyone already knows that neither man's legal expedients nor his wisdom suffice to control the world of his experience: famine, earthquake, violence – these are outside his dominion. Only God is competent here, and given the liberty he has woven into the fabric of his creation all he can do is restrain it within acceptable bounds. This is, to some extent of course, what Yahweh is getting at in his speeches. Texts such as 38:12ff are taken by not a few exegetes to suggest that in spite of appearances, of the seeming absurdity of the human condition, God does exercise a moral control.[17] But in fact the Yahweh Speeches (especially in 28:39–41:34) tend more to suggest that such a cosmic order is simply a theory that man himself evolved so as to control his environment. Therefore, the environment is naturally uncontrolled, and if it is to be circumscribed needs a manmade harness. It was man, not God, who created a "logical" cosmos; "order" and "reason" are fictions he imposes for his own comfort on God's world.

Thus in his response to his human interlocutor Yahweh uses, not the argument of the law-court, but an argument drawn from creation. He begins, in the first part of the first speech (38:4–38), with an argument from the human sciences: cosmogony and meteorology. But when he turns to "zoology" (38:39–39:30) a subtle change sets in.[18] Even in the "known" world of wild creatures and humans the irrational abounds, created by God, this is compounded by the fabulous world of Behemoth and Leviathan (40:15–41:34) – creatures, yes, but of the absurd, the unreasonable, the incomprehensible. One infers that God has a "reason" for the existence of these creatures – they are, after all, his handiwork: "Behold Behemoth, whom I created as I created you" (40:15). But they do not make sense – to logical man looking for an orderly creator and a just judge. Nor does the savage physical or psychological alienation that is part of the condition of man. Both, however, "make sense" to their creator.

In the Prologue the drama began by presenting an ideology, a familiar but stereotype world "in which a 'truth' is assumed about the nature of suffering and its relationship to God".[19] But his own experience has rendered this untenable for Job, so he searches for *some* other "truth" to replace the stereotype. Indeed, his very rebellion against God as traditionally understood is in essence a search, through the experience of absurdity, for an alternative concept of the divinity. He pushes his revolt to the limits of moral courage, and the fact that this rebellion is not condemned, but is given at least a limited approval as against the stereotype of the tradition (42:7), suggests that *the act of revolt itself* was the right reaction – for a prisoner of the Absurd.

Indeed, such an attitude of contestation is essential to the dramatic nature of the *Book of Job*, as it is to *Prometheus* of Aeschylus. Equally essential is the fact that no easy solution is offered by the Yahweh Speeches. Such a solution would destroy the tragic dimension of the book, and so destroy meaning. For tragedy is about the inexplicable, the paradoxical in human existence. As Steiner suggests,[20] "tragedy tells us that the purposes of men sometimes run against the grain of inexplicable and destructive forces that lie 'outside' yet very close." To ask the question "why does an innocent man suffer?" is analogous to asking why Antigone and not Creon had to die; why Oedipus and no one else was chosen for a tragic fate. Given the literary genre in question no answer is possible. Were any answer given the "problem" at the heart of the play would be the relatively simple one of innocent suffering. Likewise, the *mashal* genre of the book cannot afford an answer, for the question is not one of innocence or guilt: it is about the kind of God who allows suffering. The Job of the Dialogue had one answer. The God of the Theophany has another – the suggestion that Yahweh is not a judge who measures out reward or punishment as "deserved". He is a poet, an artist for whom suffering is a necessary catalyst for creativity. It is therefore a positive element in life, one that is

126

essential to the creation of something true or beautiful. Pain is closely akin to the divine discontent of the creative artist. And it makes one think: about life, about meaning, about God himself – things normally taken for granted, as if a life without the absurdity of innocent suffering were in some way whole or authentic. A world in which no lion killed to survive, in which no eagle soared in dispute of the laws of logic, would not be a world of wonder. Only one who believes that a "perfect" and "reasonable" world existed, a world in which everything could be explained and fitted together like a jigsaw, could formulate the principle that a just God could not be responsible for suffering. But there is a different kind of God: the one Job meets in the Theophany – the divine poet.

Job's new concept of God

Thus the gratuitous, and indeed "unjust" suffering imposed on Job in the Prologue points beyond the stereotype solution to the reality of God – as he sees himself. The protagonist is not told that Yahweh is just or that suffering can be explained. Neither is true for the dramatist. Through the double experience of his own suffering (Dialogue) and the God-vision (Theophany) he comes to know the divinity, for suffering is part of the Creator's scheme of things; part of the creation that is Yahweh's act of self-expression; part of the totality that reflects his relationship with what he has created. Not to suffer means to be part-human, for one crucial element of the relationship God-world, poet–poem has not been experienced. God does not simply *allow* absurdity – it is an aspect of the whole he created and is essential to its beauty. One might say, in the light of what Yahweh shows Job in the Theophany, that some form of alienation or un-reason represents the birth-pangs that necessarily accompany the divine poem of the world. In a perceptive essay on religious poetry Helen Gardner suggests that perhaps Job and Deutero-Isaiah represent the first break in the traditional theology that "suffering is a mark of divine displeasure".[21]

127

The calculus of whether suffering is related to sin is one that becomes a judge, not a poet. Discovering "the kind of God who allows the innocent to suffer", the *Book of Job* evolves a new theology of suffering, and a new concept of God: pain is the creative dimension of the divine artist. The reader of the whole book, with its two arguments, is forced to ask: which is more truly human – Eliphaz's argument that suffering is "deserved in some way", or the idea that it is the divine catalyst in the creation of some new aspect of eternal truth, something that adds beauty to creation?

Job had expected, and indeed in the Dialogue projected, a God of justice. In the Theophany Yahweh shows himself as a God who created mystery – a category broader than the judicial. He presents himself as poet, and invites man to accept the poetry of life and its concomitant suffering. In the Dialogue man achieves his stature: with unshaken integrity he questions the God of theology. In the Theophany Yahweh demonstrates *his* stature: his is a divinity wider in its dispositions than the forms of reason allow. He places before Job a vision of world "order", but an order that makes no sense because it is beyond the capacity of human reason. Suffering, unreason, absurdity itself is part of this order, not a negation of it. One either accepts this or finds a substitute God. The God of the Theophany is the divinity as he sees himself, and that is obviously the kind of God who allows predator and prey to occupy the same living space; the kind of God who creates "useless" creatures, who takes pleasure in absurdity by enjoying ugly and dangerous beings – in brief, one who delights in the fabulous.

Yahweh shows his real nature in chapters 38–41, a nature previously ignored by Job and the friends who, all of them, represent the human side of things, the refusal to allow God have a mysterious, dark side. This is natural, for the human creature is driven by a god-given urge to *know* what the dark side of existence is like.[22] Hence the tension in man, a creature living in an alien world not chosen by himself. Both Job and the friends oversimplify the human predicament. God's world cannot be explained by logic, for God is beyond logic. There is always mystery at the heart of existence. Birth, death and that half-way house, suffering; what "meaning" is there to any of these? The fact that one is a joyous phenomenon makes it no more *reasonable* than if it were unhappy.

No aspect of creation is in itself either good or bad – it is "good" to the extent that it forms an environment within which the individual can achieve something. Human existence is necessarily contingent; what gives it value is the way one reacts to it. This is a new "theodicy" offered by Yahweh in his response. Had the friends been aware of it that might have saved them from interpreting divinity in terms familiar to themselves. Even Job had suffered from such a fixed vision, and perhaps this lies behind the text of his speech in 21:7–18 – uncannily prescient in the light of the Theophany.

> Why do the wicked live,
>   reach old age, and grow mighty in power?
> Their children are established in their presence,
>   and their offspring before their eyes.
> Their houses are safe from fear,
>   and no rod of God is upon them.
> Their bull breeds without fail;
>   their cow calves, and does not cast her calf.
> They send forth their little ones like a flock,
>   and their children dance.
> They sing to the tambourine and the lyre,
>   and rejoice to the sound of the pipe.
> They spend their days in prosperity,
>   and in peace they go down to Sheol.
> They say to God, "Depart from us!
>   We do not desire the knowledge of thy ways.
> What is the Almighty, that we should serve him?
>   And what profit do we get if we pray to him?"
> Behold, is not their prosperity in their hand?
>   The counsel of the wicked is far from me.
>
> How often is it that the lamp of the wicked is put out?
>   That their calamity comes upon them?
>   That God distributes pains in his anger?
> That they are like straw before the wind,
>   and like chaff that the storm carries away?

This is, significantly, a wisdom poem and it presents a moral implication to the "perceived un-order" of the Cosmos. God allows absurdity to exist in the world, as he demonstrates in chapters 38–41, but while Job seems to see it in terms of a "law of disorder" Yahweh sees it as a "fact of un-order". While this tells something about the human condition as perceived, it says more about God. He is one who has created darkness as well as light, pain as well as joy.

"What kind of God?" is the question the Prologue puts to the reader, who is left to choose between the alternatives offered – Job's argument and God's. This openness to interpretation is no small virtue in the *Book of Job*, but perhaps no less important is what it has contributed to theological method. Had Yahweh not spoken on his own behalf the Dialogue, standing alone, would represent a forceful existential statement. By intervening, God confers legitimacy on the method adopted by Job in the first and most passionate part of the book, whose great contribution is the fact that it brings theology out of its prison by opening it up to doubt about its sufficiency. This is done by the fact that Job rigorously applies human reason to the received data of traditional theology about God. It brings a "layman's perspective" to official faith, which is no longer to be seen as a deposit simply to be accepted. Without a traditional theology of a just God and the fable of an innocent man suffering there would be no articulation of the tension between faith and human experience, no new theology of suffering, and no new theological method of rational enquiry. It is evident that two characters dominate the drama, Job and Yahweh; and therefore two "theologies", that of man and that of God. The third "theology", the seminary dogmatics of the friends, is of little value except as a foil. Not that it is a bad theology – in fact it is presented with sensitivity and delicacy – but there inevitably comes a stage in thinking man's journey through life when classical theology is inadequate to meet the needs of a specific experience of alienation. The "new" theological method forces the reader to look more closely at his traditional views of God, and indeed it deflects his attention from a too close concern with ethics and human destiny, directing it instead to God *as he is in himself*: transcendent, incomprehensible, irreducible to the schematization of theology manuals.[23] Pascal rightly saw this fact when he said that God is by nature so much a hidden God that any religion that claimed to know him, and any religion that did not respect reason, was deceptive.

NOTES

1. R.M. Polzin, "The Framework of the Book of Job", in *Interpretation* 28(1974), 195. See also R. Gordis, *The Book of Job*.
2. MacKenzie, "The Purpose of the Yahweh Speeches in the Book of Job". Alonso Schökel, in his commentary *Job*, takes seriously the idea that the whole book was intended to be read as a whole.
3. For a discussion of the purpose and style of the Theophany see among others, E.M. Good, *Irony in the Old Testament*, Sheffield, 1981; J.G. Williams, "Comedy, Irony, Intercession: A Few Notes in Response", in *Semeia* 7(1977), 140; A. Lacocque, "Job or the Importance of Religion and Philosophy", in *Semeia* 19(1981), 33–52.
4. N.C. Habel, *Book of Job*, 562. Also F.J. Bolton, "The Sense of the Text and a New Vision", in *Semeia* 19(1981), 89, and Lacocque in the same issue of *Semeia*.
5. The Hebrew text uses two words deliberately to conjure up the "lawsuit" imagery: "to contend", *harob*, comes from the familiar root *rib*, "lawsuit", and "the accuser", *moiah*, is another forensic term. See also Habel, *Job*, 548f.
6. L. Dornisch discusses this idea in "The Book of Job and Ricoeur's Hermeneutics", in *Semeia* 19,12. Ricoeur himself suggests a concrete image *followed* by a question, but this is not quite accurate in the light of the text and its structure. See M.V. Fox in the same issue, 58.
7. See Bolton, "The Sense of the Text", 88; J.J. Collins, "Proverbial Wisdom and the Yahwist Vision", in *Semeia* 17(1980), 5, and Habel, *Job*, 53.
8. M. Nussbaum, *The Fragility of Goodness. Luck and Ethics in Greek Tragedy and Philosophy*, Cambridge, 1986, 25f., discusses this whole idea, citing Sartre's *Les Mouches* as an example of evasion, In the same work, 81, she discusses strife as constitutive of values in relation to *Antigone*.
9. D. Robertson, *The Old Testament and the Literary Critic*, 51.
10. S. Terrien, *Job*, 18; See also M.H. Pope, *Job*, xiv, H.H. Rowley, *Job*, 28f., and J.E. Hartley, *The Book of Job*, 67.
11. This is effectively the position taken by Eliphaz in chapters 4–5, as Ravasi, *Giobbe*, 57, points out. It is interesting to note how this speech signals the future "God-argument" of the Theophany, though the theologian does not draw out the logical conclusion.
12. A very interesting study of Hemingway shows up this particular point of what might be called a secular theology, in C. Brooks, *The Hidden God. Studies in Hemingway, Faulkner, Yeats, Eliot and Warren*, New Haven, 1963, 21.

13. A. MacLeish, *J.B. A Play in Verse*, Boston, 1956, scene II.
14. G. Steiner, *The Death of Tragedy*, London, 1961, 15. Ravasi, *Giobbe*, 68, agrees that the starting point for Job and the friends, at least with regard to God, was the same.
15. See L. Dornisch, "The Book of Job and Ricoeur's Hermeneutics", 15. See also Alonso Schökel, *Job*, 604, for the idea that Job had wanted to be proved innocent and was.
16. P. Nemo, *Job et l'excès du mal*, 121. See also J. Vermeylen, *Job, ses amis et son Dieu. La Légende de Job et ses relectures postexiliques*, Leiden, 1986, 40.
17. Habel, *Job*, 532, Hartley, *Book of Job*, 497. Vermeylen, *Job, ses amis*, 51f.
18. R. Alter, *The Art of Biblical Poetry*, 104, sees it all as God creating the world, setting it in motion and taking care of it – an argument that is relatively common. However, 38:39 seems rather to signal a change of emphasis.
19. Dornisch, "The Book of Job and Ricoeur's Hermeneutics", 20f.
20. Steiner, *Death of Tragedy*, 128f. See also a treatment of this whole point of view of responsibility and suffering in A. Feuillet, "L'énigme de la souffrance et la réponse de Dieu", in *Dieu Vivant* 17(1950), 79f.
21. H. Gardner, *Religion and Literature*, Oxford, 1971, 60, is discussing tragic catharsis and the purging of the passions in tragedy by a reference to W.B. Yeats, who said that the image of Yahweh is one of terror, but a terror so magnificent that the beauty of the idea cleanses away all pain, in so doing intensifying the feeling of beauty.
22. This idea is well expressed in Qoh. 3:10–11 where man's urge to know is frustrated by his natural inability to do. See also Ravasi, *Giobbe*, 773f. On the moral effects of this idea of "good for authenticity" see Lacocque, "Job or the Impotence of Religion", 38, and G. von Rad, *Wisdom in Israel*, London, 1972, 253f, who suggests that perhaps Sirach's approach is the best: that of "and-both". Things are sometimes good and sometimes bad, and must be grasped according to their proper time. Sometimes from man's point of view what God sends is bad, sometimes good, and even God's direct intervention in the world of man can be perceived as bad.
23. H. Knight, "Job, considered as a contribution to Hebrew Theology", in *SJTh* 9(1956), 73. See this point in his *Pensées*, Paris, 1946, 29f.
24. J. Lévêque, *Job et son Dieu. Essai d'eségèse et de théologie biblique*, Paris, 1970, 689.

PART IV

THE EPILOGUE: 42:7–17
RETURN TO REALITY

Chapter 8

Going back into the night

God has not had the last word. That is the author's privilege. The dramatic structure of the work makes it clear that the book cannot end simply with the rather ambiguous "submission" of the protagonist. Literary unity would demand the same kind of rounding-off, of return to prosperity that was common to this sort of writing in the ancient Near East. The final author–editor of *Job* supplies this in the Epilogue, a "happy ending", but with a twist of genius worthy of the book it closes.

The Epilogue

The Epilogue, no less than the Prologue and for much the same reasons, poses many questions of authenticity and structure for the scholar.

What first strikes the reader are the obvious discrepancies of character and topic. The Satan, who played so crucial a role in the Prologue, is nowhere mentioned. Nor is Job's wife, who had served as an important catalyst for the second editorial confirmation of Job's integrity (2:9f). Besides this, there appear to be two distinct "epilogues". Chapter 42:7–9 is clearly meant to close the poetic dialectic of Dialogue and Theophany. The opening words of this prose section are clearly meant to serve as an editorial link with the Theophany: "After Yahweh had spoken these words to Job" (v. 7a), while v. 7b, which re-introduces the three friends, recalls the Dialogue: "Yahweh said to

135

Eliphaz the Temanite, 'I burn with anger against you and your two friends because you did not speak of me what was right, as my servant Job did' ". Dialogue and Theophany are thus presented by the editor as a literary unit.

In the second section, vv. 10–17, none of these characters appears, and the only link seems to be the use of the divine name "Yahweh". We are introduced instead to Job's brothers and sisters who have never been heard of before this, yet who now, in his moment of rehabilitation, fill the consolatory role previously filled, in sorrow, by the friends (2:11). Also, Job's "restoration" is here described with the mathematical accuracy so beloved of the story-teller as exactly *double* the material goods he lost in chapter 1: "fourteen thousand sheep, six thousand camels, a thousand yoke of oxen, a thousand she-asses". Even the narrative hyperbole is identical. What both these "minor epilogues" share, however, is a return to the patriarchal style and folk-tale atmosphere of the Prologue.

The editorial intention behind this combined prose Epilogue of 42:7–17 is evident. The first section of vv. 7–9 resolves the tension of Dialogue–Theophany by acknowledging both Yahweh's answer and his approval of Job's argument, thereby definitively framing the poetic Job–God sections within the prose narrative framework of Prologue and Epilogue. Verses 10–17 now return us to the world of fable with which we began in chapters 1–2, effectively bringing down the curtain.

Returning to reality

Despite its problematic nature, the Epilogue is necessary to the drama of the *Book of Job*, and the final editor who gave us the whole book in its present form knew his dramatic values. After his travail, and his experience of the God-argument, Job is forced to go back into the real world he inhabited before ever Yahweh and the Satan entered his life. He returns to the world of everyday living – it is the same but he is not. He is a different person, capable of bringing a new maturity and a more open mind

136

to the human situation of life in the world. In the first verses of the Prologue he was no more than a type, too good to be true, too perfect to mean much to everyday folk. His experience of absurdity brought him down to ordinary level, while his experience of God added a new, hitherto undreamed of, dimension:

> With the hearing of the ear I had heard of you,
> but now my eyes have seen you . . .

(42:5)

and this sends him back to the world of reality with a new perspective that makes him more capable of understanding life. He is now a real human being.

The reason for the Epilogue would seem to be the exigence of the dramatic art rather than the demands of the argument. For, logically, suffering is not reversible; even God cannot "restore the fortunes" of one who has lost his family and suffered physical and psychological misfortune (42:10). Giving Job as many children as he had before ("seven sons and three daughters": 42:13 and 1:2) does not compensate for or negate the loss of the first ten (2:18f). The question that will always remain in the mind is the "why?" of the *first* tragedy – why such meaningless suffering; "what kind of God is capable of doing this?" The friends do not see this point; their repeated argument (5:8; 8:21; 11:13; 22:21) – "repent, pray even, and God will restore you" will never make up for what God has already done, much less explain it. But the audience sees this point, and as the curtain goes down on the tragedy the reader, like the Job of the Epilogue, goes back into the dark, wet night of reality to cope, on his part, with the human condition. Job's argument had been valid, as Yahweh admitted; he had "spoken what was right" about the divinity (42:7). After hearing God's side of it he submits, tacitly accepting the validity of the divine argument.

The reader has heard both sides of the *mashal*, and now he must put Job's rational argument and Yahweh's convincing one together and work it out for himself. Just *what* kind of God must man deal with?

The God of Job and the God of the reader

The figure of God in the *Book of Job* is a masterpiece of fluidity, a kaleidoscope of changing images and colours. Never once from beginning to end is the concept "God" static, except for the friends – and their understanding of divinity never moves from the purely traditional idea of a loving God, sovereign creator and just judge. But God has many more faces than that, as both Job and the reader come to realize.

All begin with the same preconception – Job, friends and reader. All initially share the traditional image of "God" inherited through faith, and all "fear God and turn away from evil" as Job did in the Prologue (1:1). All are religious people according to a common tradition, and in that tradition the concept "god" is fixed: he is the originator and just co-ordinator of the world, which he preserves. But while the friends never surrender this monolithic view, the reader's perception changes throughout, as this "god-concept" comes into conflict with the "real god" of human suffering and experience. The God of Job in the Prologue is familiar and remains so throughout the speeches of the friends. This is a god who has been captured by the traditional clichés and so can be approached and "understood" through the traditional channels – prayer, submission and sacrifice. This is the God of the untroubled believer: "Job would send and sanctify his children, and he would rise early in the morning and offer burnt offerings according to the number of them all; for Job said, 'It may be that my sons have sinned, and cursed God in their hearts.' Thus Job did continually." In the Epilogue he has become a divinity who seems both to repudiate that image and to uphold it: he rebukes the friends for defending it, yet imposes the traditional ritual of prayer, submission and sacrifice on them. Within the book one concept of "god" is being continually played-off against the other at all levels of the debate. The "god" known by Job in the Prologue is that of the friends. Over against this, in stark contrast, is the existential "god" of Job in the Dialogue, the "God's god" of the Theophany and the "god" of Job and the friends in the Epilogue. Thus many images of the divinity are presented in the book, but it requires the reader's double-vision – of Job's experience of unjust suffering (Dialogue) and God's own view of himself (Theophany) – to see that all these are simply different faces of the same God. Various as they are, they are all valid images of a divinity that carefully avoids definition. One notices, in fact, how even the *names* of God in the Dialogue are interchangeable: El, Eloah, Shaddai, and these are set over against the "Yahweh" of the Prologue and Epilogue. Both Job and friends are right – and wrong; even Yahweh's own image of himself as poet/artist is right, though the reader can never be sure he has grasped precisely what God is revealing about himself in the divine speeches. The fact is that God *as he is* cannot be grasped mentally by either traditional categories or categories born of experience. The friends, by holding grimly to the traditional concept, have in fact annexed God, limited his infinite capacity to *be* many things. Holders of a monolithic tradition often do. Job has understood divinity better than they: in his revolt he has recognised that God is arbitrary, and is responsible for suffering.

There is no one fixed, image of God. No tradition can embrace the reality, for experience reveals the multi-faceted nature of the divinity. "Belief about God" can be inherited – Job's faith in the Prologue was, and that of the friends is throughout. But *religion* must be based on some personal experience of God. Every religious individual finds God in his own experience, whatever that be: joy, or pain, or alienation; and for this reason his concept of God is shaped by that experience. Each one may thus have a different "image" of God, whose nature is not fixed or limited by any *one* tradition. True, many things remain common to all – much of the traditional portrait endures for Job and friends – but the tradition has been, and is for the reader, a limited concept, a lowest common denominator, and must be fleshed-out and expanded by human experience. "God" is a wider concept, and a more flexible, than any one category. In fact, for the Hebrew "knowledge of God" pertains to the realm of experience, not to conceptual thinking alone. The friends have at best a "notional" understanding of theology which has fixed "truths". Job has a real understanding of God.

In his relationship with man God has always used the language of human experience and imagination.[24] He addresses the individual on the level of imagination, within the categories of experience. Justice, joy, love – certainly; but also shame, guilt, suffering, slavery. These are all "words" that communicate an "image" of God, and indeed are words that are basic to the teaching dimension of proverb and parable. God supplies some words and images, but man forges many others for himself from his experience. This is the real anguish Job faces in the Dialogue: the images of God he forges from his experience seem to contradict the images supplied by his theological tradition. The friends know a God of justice, but Job has experienced an unjust God; they know a God of love, he has experienced a God who is "hunter of man" (10:16). The fact is that God is all of these. In some way he is in all he has created, and his face can be seen in all he has created.

Throughout the *Book of Job* both types of god–language have been deliberately preserved side by side: the traditional images and the images born of harsh experience (e.g. chap. 8 and chap. 10). The God of justice and love is presented side by side with the God of arbitrary suffering, for both are the "real" God – or rather, the real God, Yahweh's own "god", comprises both. To a great extent one could begin with 42:7, where God himself agrees with Job's assessment of him – as a God of absurdity: "the Lord said to Eliphaz the Temanite, 'my wrath is kindled against you and against your two friends; for you have not spoken of me what is right, as my servant Job has' ". The protagonist of the Dialogue did not know the Yahweh of the Theophany, but the reader has met both. Both "gods" are linked by absurdity, for Yahweh's "god" is as absurd as Job's. The reader sees both side by side. The core of Job's experience remains the reality of his unexplained suffering and the silence of the only one who could have explained it, Yahweh himself. It was the intensity of Job's anger against the silent divinity that finally provoked God's answer – for he recognized himself in Job's picture of him. What makes a caricature bite is its unpleasant likeness to its subject. God is indeed a God who has planned suffering right from the moment of creation (10:13). Job sees it negatively at first, but viewed positively it means that suffering is part of the *grace* of creation, inserted into creation and integral to it. The common believer expects everything to go relatively smoothly for him; even though he lives in a world of suffering he does not expect it to touch *him*. How could it? He is after all an averagely decent person and God does not strike out at such as he – he is not like that. But experience shows that all around him are a number of "averagely decent people" whose children die; who cannot have children they long for; who are incurably ill, like the author of Ps. 88. This is as much the "real world" as the first, as much part of reality as Job's initial *shalom* and the continuing *shalom* of the friends. And God is as much responsible for one as for the other. Has reality, or God, changed because Job was stricken and his friends not?

Believers tend to limit the range of god-experience. For the friends, Yahweh could not be met positively in suffering, for he was "not that kind of God". He could only be met negatively for he was by definition "just" and so innocent suffering could not be part of his plan. One could not "see his face" in pain, it simply was not part of the way he dealt with his friends. The Job of the Prologue could still mouth pieties: "The Lord gave, and the Lord has taken away; blessed be the name of the Lord", for he had suffered only superficially, really. At the other end the Epilogue shows the equally conventional "god of the happy ending". Neither speaks to the reader. If he suffers it is the rebel of chapters 3–31 that speaks his language. And God came to Job directly, in his revolt. The world as it is, as it has been created in all its mysterious diversity, is the mediator of God. But the Epilogue does show that the Yahweh of the mysterious universe was the same as the God of the traditional faith and piety of the Prologue. No one image of God, particularly the fixed concept of traditional faith, is adequate to communicate his reality.

Perhaps the *Book of Job*, more than any other book, liberates religion from the fixed formulae of god-language, and serves as a necessary antidote to the rather too human God of the prophets and the historical traditions of the Old Testament: one who becomes angry, one who loves, one who wages war. Someone rather like us, whom we can understand! But God is transcendent. No one image is sufficient – good, just, true are human categories. No theologian can define his nature in a formula or an image – in the last analysis not even the words of the poet are adequate to express his reality.

INDEX